Chronicles Of Jane

THE JANE PRINT

KAMELAH BLAIR

Copyright © 2020 Kamelah Blair

All rights reserved. Printed in the United States of America.

No part of this book may be used or reproduced in any manner whatsoever without written permission except in the case of brief quotations embodied in critical articles or reviews

ISBN: 979-8-66420-205-2

Published by: Daughter of the King Publishing

Farrah Hodgson
Daughter of the King Publishing

DEDICATION

To my two kings. Not only have you made me proud to see the young men you've become, but I am also proud of the woman you've made me become. Love, Mom.

CONTENTS

	Kamelah Blair	i
1	Blueprint	1
2	The Foundation	16
3	Developing Without Materials	24
4	Instability Before The Fall	42
5	The Engineers	55
6	Wisdom Builds A House	67
7	Cracks In The Foundation	73
8	Rebuilding The Foundation	84
9	The PLAN	105
10	The Phone Call	112

KAMELAH BLAIR

The phoenix rising from the ashes depicts who Kamelah Blair is. She was born and raised in Toronto, Ontario, and lived within the community of Jane and Finch. Jane Street was a tightknit, urban community that had a mix of middle- and upper-class families, who were filled with intelligence and street smarts.

Kamelah is the CEO of four successful companies, and a mother of two. She graduated from George Brown College with an Honors Diploma in Medical Administration and Blood Lab Technician.

The stone that the builders refused was what she used to build her empire. She is known as the black sheep on her mother's side of the family, and the only college graduate on her father's side of the family. Her uncle, grandmother, godmother, father, and stepmother encouraged her to be better than the negative things that were said to her.

CHAPTER ONE:

BLUEPRINT

Jane is not a person. Jane is a street and also a lifestyle. Growing up, Jane was just a place for me. Over the years, it changed. But it meant home to me. When I'm on the highway, and I hear the road sounds, a peace comes over me, because I know that I'm close to Jane and Finch. It's a breath of fresh air. When I'm anywhere else, I'm uptight; I don't know what it is. Jane Street is where I belong. It's home to me. As I grew older, I gained a certain strength and boldness that I believe I inherited from living down the lane. When I got a little bit older, and lived on my own, I lived in Driftwood. These are all rival areas, but I also have connections in these places, so I hung out on both sides of Jane. In my eyes, Jane is one big community. I don't think of it any other way. In my time, it was just home. At one point, I was very mindful of not going on the south side of Jane. But whether I'm in the south side or north side of Jane, the area doesn't define me. I am Jane Street. At the end of the day, it is my home. Jane is where I was raised, and it is where I got my experience. It is where I learned to be me. It impacted who I am and how I see the world. Jane is my personal Encyclopedia.

The journey begins with my parents—Yanks my father, and Goldy my mother—a young married couple living a street life. Both of my parents grew up in Jamaica, met there, and fell in love there. My mother and my father have different stories about how they came in contact with each other. They migrated to Canada in the early 1970s, and started their families here. My mother gave birth to me in the month of September. Unlike my parents, I was born and raised in the area of Jane and Finch. Although I am the eldest of thirteen children within the family, I was the only child for an extended period of time. However, I was not alone. Not only did I have my parents, but I also considered some of my neighbours and my friends as my family. I had my godmother, Helen, my Auntie Pat, and my uncles Jah-Jah and Randy. We were a very tight-knit community. Growing up, I didn't live with my parents alone, because the street life was what they lived. Over time, they separated, but they remained legally married. I never understood it, but to each his own.

In my early years, I lived with my mother and father. My first memory of my parents being together was when Yanks was getting arrested. I was between the ages of five and seven when I witnessed my parents physically fighting. It all started when my mother stole some drugs from my father to give to her boyfriend. I knew in my heart that she was being unfaithful to him; her actions made it clear. Father had come home consumed with anger towards her and, without hesitation, confronted my mother about the drugs that she had stolen. I vividly recall that he was wearing a brown sweater with dark brown elbows and a button-up shirt underneath, and his locks were cut low. I knew what my mother had done, but I did not want to say anything, because I was already being abused physically and verbally by her, and they had had a fight prior to this event because of what my mother was doing to me. My mother, of course, wanted to put the blame on me, because she could envision the rage that my father would have towards her if he found out the truth. Well, that is exactly what she did—she pinned it on me. My mother was adamant that I had taken the drugs. However, as a child, I had a clear understanding of what drugs was, and I instinctively knew it was something terrible. Therefore, I did not touch it. Nevertheless, my mother used that excuse to get my father to leave. At the time, we lived at Jane and Trethewey. Across from Jane and Trethewey, there was a Metro Housing building that had about five floors. It had a long hallway that was big enough to accommodate several units. Miss Rose, who was my babysitter and the crossing guard at the time, lived on the second floor, the same floor as my parents. However, we lived on opposite ends of the long hallway. I would spend most of my time at her house, because I wanted to escape from my mother. The physical and verbal abuse wasn't beneficial to my growth and mental development. You have to actually be in a situation like mine, or similar, to know what I am articulating. Ann, my mother's friend, lived on the first floor, and my father's best friend, Jermaine, and his girlfriend, Diana, lived on the fourth floor. Diana was a beautiful lady, five-feet-five with fair skin, and Jermaine was a tall, muscular, dark-skinned man who took a lot of street drugs, including uppers and downers medication, which affected his emotions and mood swings.

One day, I was disobedient to my mother, because she wanted me to stay inside, but I did not want to do that. I had asked to play at Jermaine and Diana's house, as they had young children as well, and they were my playmates, but Goldy said "No." I decided to use reverse psychology, and I asked her if I could go to Miss Rose's house. I had on a baby blue dress with polka dots and a touch of red at the collar, and my hair was in pigtails. As soon as she said "yes," I ran down the hallway, and as I was running down the hallway, I looked back and there she was, my mother, peeking out to make sure I was going to my babysitter's apartment. When I heard the door close, I took the staircase and went to my friends' house. I brought some toys with me, including Barbie dolls and Jem and the Holograms. When I entered Jermaine and Diana's place, Diana was still on crutches from an altercation she had a few weeks prior. I did not witness the dispute between them; however, I had heard the neighbourhood mothers talking about it, and my friend and I had also had a little discussion about what had transpired.

Suddenly, while we were playing, Jermaine came inside upset, and went into the kitchen to get a beer. He and Diana started to argue, and he pulled out a cleaver on her. I heard him saying, "If you don't stop lying,

I'm going to cut your hand." Eventually, he did cut her hand on the freezer door, and she came into the living room with her hand wrapped up in a brown paper towel. I was petrified, and I told him that I was going home. He said, "No, you can't." I responded immediately, "But I don't live here!" Jermaine wasn't operating as a normal man at all. He clearly didn't like my response; I saw it in his facial expression. He was furious to the point where he put Diana, the children, and me in their bedroom, locked the door, and then walked out into the living room area with no remorse expressed. The children started to cry. Their crying revealed to me that this was a regular behaviour of his. They were used to seeing them fight, but you could have seen that this example of a man and a woman's relationship was far from their acceptance. Fifteen minutes passed, and Jermaine came back into the room and asked us if we wanted a snack. I declined and told him that I just wanted to go home. He said, "Sorry, Tiny, I cannot do that." Tiny is a nickname that I had as a child. As he said that, he did not look upset; instead, he had a pleasant demeanor. Nevertheless, that didn't prevent him from locking the four of us in the closet. At that point, I said to myself, *"I should've listened to my mom and just stayed home."* Being in the closet was not the best feeling. The closet was dark, and I felt scared to death. The words of my mother were on repeat in my mind. I definitely should have listened to her.

We were all in there for an exceptionally long time, and then he came for us. He then put us in the closet in their bedroom. The furniture in the room was all wood, and it was expensive back in the day. I saw that they had a small TV, and it was on top of the chest of drawers. As I was observing their room, Jermaine transferred us into the next room, and then he proceeded to the washroom. While he was in the washroom, we came up with an escape strategy, quickly seized the moment, and ran off. It actually felt as if we had escaped from being kidnapped. It made no sense going to the second floor where I lived, so instead, we went to the first floor where Ann lived. By the time we got to the first floor, we could hear him coming down the steps.

We were so scared that we hid at the bottom of the steps where the storage area was. Ann was playing loud music; therefore, she did not hear us screaming, and Metro Housing buildings had thin walls and were not built in the best way. He eventually found us, and we had to go back into their unit. While passing Miss Rose's door, we yelled and screamed, but yet she couldn't catch on to us either. I was not sure what she was doing that day. There we were again, kidnapped. I use the word kidnapped to describe his actions because, to me, that was what it felt like. He put us back into their bedroom for another fifteen minutes, and locked the door. During this time, water was falling off of Jermaine's body, and Diana had a fountain flowing from her eyes. They both seemed to be scared, but Jermaine's scared was another type of scared, the one where you would do anything, and that includes committing murder. Being present in an atmosphere like theirs, all I wanted to say was, "You can keep my toys. All I want to do is go home. We passed my home coming here." But the words never came out of my mouth, even though I said it over and over in my mind.

His demeanour started to change, and he started to call Diana degrading names, like "bitch" and "whore." He mentioned my mother in that manner as well. They went back and forth for roughly over an hour. He then proceeded to say to her, "You, Goldy, and your other friends say bad things about me! What do you have to say to me now? You're not cleaning up the house, and you're not doing anything!" Jermaine and Diana continued to argue. Suddenly, he pushed her against the chest of drawers. And then he asked her, "Are you going to tell me the truth?"

She replied, "I don't know what you're talking about. What do you want to say to me now?"

He then turned to us, the children he held captive. We were standing, bundled together in fear on the other side of the room. He looked directly at us and said, "This is what happens when you are with a man, and you tell him a lie." He took out a gun from the waist of his pants, pointed the end of the gun to her head, and pulled the trigger. Just like that, he killed her with one shot, right through the TV. Time froze. I was speechless. When I came back to reality, I immediately became aware that the kids were crying, and I began to console them, yes, in my devastated state. This situation had caused me pain, but it also taught me how to nurture others. In that jiffy, all I had in me was a hug. I literally had no words of comfort. I hugged them so tightly that there was no space for air to pass through. Their world had just crumbled right in front of them. I was not a fat child, neither was I skinny, yet our bones connected with each other so quickly. We truly were in need of each other's comfort. Hurt flooded our young souls. It was a traumatizing experience that I would wish on absolutely no one.

I do not know when Jermaine left the apartment, but he went to the second floor, where we lived. My mother, who was pregnant at the time, opened the door for him willingly, not knowing what was going on. He was welcome to our house anytime. She left his presence to use the washroom, and he decided to shoot after her. She fell beside her canopy-style bed and went underneath. And she stayed there.

My mother said the only reason she opened the door for him was that he was my dad's best friend. He went to the other lady's floor, and started to shoot after her. I do not know whether she got shot in her leg or her ankle. Then he went to the first floor, where Ann lived, the same apartment we attempted to go to the first time. He ended up shooting her in her shoulder. He was coming back upstairs, and the building was in a complete ruckus, as people were knocking on the door. I was still in my frozen state. Not long after all this occurred, he committed suicide. Afterwards, I did not speak for a year. Not only was I mute, but I also began to sleepwalk. And to think this was all because of my dad's best friend's drug problems.

In the year 1985, after the incident, my brother was born. Not long after, I was sent to Jamaica for a holiday, because I was not speaking.

While I was there, I always had flashbacks of what I could have done differently. I lost contact with Diana's daughters, but I always missed them as my friends and thought about them often, since we all bore witness to the incident that happened in our community. I always wondered how they felt knowing it was their mother that had passed away right in front of their eyes. I told my dad, back in 2019, that I resented him, but I love my dad so dearly. I resented him because it was his best friend, and he didn't do anything. My father said to me, "There's nothing I could've done regarding the situation, because he took his own life. If he had not taken his own life, of course, I would have done something." When my dad's best friend had cut his baby mother's hand, I should've observed what was going on, but then again, I was a child, and I didn't believe the adult stories that my mother and her friends spoke about, which included stories about my father. I brushed off what my mother and her friends were doing. As a child, it never enticed me to get involved in grown folks' conversation. That was when I learned, even to this day, to observe every situation thoroughly. I tend to overthink, and I watch every situation from start to finish. That situation caused me to start behaving in this manner. We continued to live in that same apartment complex for a short period of time, then I eventually went to live in Malton with my godmother, Helen. Malton was a high-class neighbourhood, like Richmond Hill, at the time.

I had the best of both worlds. I had the privilege of experiencing a ghetto life—the drugs, the killing, the arguments, and the fast money—and I also got to live a life like *The Fresh Prince of Bel-Air*—a high-class life. Helen was a Jamaican-born woman of principles and standards. She was a nurse and an entrepreneur. She was five-feet-five, with a full head of hair and a soft-spoken voice. She was God-fearing, loving, caring, and ambitious. When I would get in trouble, her style of discipline would be to make me iron all the laundry and peel a sack of potatoes. After finishing my punishment, she would then sit me down in the second family room. She would explain my actions and the reason for my punishment, and then she would ask me, "What would you do differently?" This question allowed me to reflect on my actions. Her disciplinary skills have helped to develop me into the woman I am becoming today.

Helen was a happy lady, and that was displayed all the time in her home. She kept me busy with ballet, tap, jazz, and gymnastics. We had a dog named Harlem, and two birds. One of the birds was green and yellow, and the other was blue and yellow. My life was more structured, and I did not suffer any trauma. In Helen's home, there was an eight-foot grandfather clock, and at the bottom of the clock was storage. At that tragic time, I could hide in the bottom part of that clock or I would sit in front of it and watch time go by. She allowed me to do it, and never asked questions. She would sometimes bring my blanket to me or ask me if I wanted a snack. It was an escape for me whenever I went to my godmother's house. We ate around the table together, cooked together, and baked together. It was more like *The Cosby Show* kind of setting. I learned about love, and I felt it from her. My mother, on the other hand, never showed me that type of love. It felt as if I wasn't important to her. My dad showed and taught me love, and he preached to me daily, despite his lifestyle. However, when I was with my dad, I was never at ease, because I would always have to look over my shoulder.

One faithful day, prior to living with Helen, the police came looking for my father. He had on a blue, red, and gray slacks and a gray shirt. His undershirt was showing and, by now, he had started to grow back his dreadlocks. He threw me on his back, piggyback style, and he took six flights of stairs. When we reached the sixth floor, the police were looking for a man that fit my dad's description. They said his government name as well as his aliases over the Walkie-talkies. My father started to knock on random doors. I will never forget that a little lady came out, and he asked her, while pulling out some money, "Can you just watch her for an hour?" At first, she looked startled, and then she just said, "Okay."

The police were on the third floor coming up. I was there for about three or four hours, but the lady didn't eat sugar, so she couldn't offer me sweets. And she didn't watch TV, so we just sat and listened to the radio. Breaking news came on, and I heard my dad's name. She looked at me, but I never looked up; I just acted like I did not know the name. They said something along the lines of an incident happening in that area, but I didn't react to it. Again, I did not say anything, because that was the way of the streets. Then I heard someone knock on the door, and it was one of my dad's friends. I ran to him, and she picked up right away that I knew him. He said, "Thanks," and he offered her more money.

She said calmly, "No, the gentleman had given me money before."
"No, take it. It's okay. We appreciate that you watched her for more than an hour."

She turned to him at the door and asked if everything was okay, and if he would like me to stay there longer. I didn't look up at her, but I smiled.

"No, it's okay. She's fine, but thanks," my father's friend said nicely.
He brought me back to my mom, and I did not see my dad for a while. He would not be present in my life for three weeks, and then it went back to normal afterwards. This happened often. I went to school in the area, and after school, we would stop at the buildings. My dad would bring me to buy a snack, and I wouldn't hesitate to get my two dollars to buy fries and gravy. Two dollars was in the form of a paper bill at the time. After leaving the store, we usually crossed the street to go home. I enjoyed doing this as a child. When all this was done, I'd take my bath, eat my dinner, and read a few books before going to bed. The frequent sound of gunshots on Jane Street triggered me. I would instantly feel water dripping off of me, and feel the need to hide. Yes, sweating is a sign of fright.

After the sleepwalking continued, my mom figured out that something was wrong with me, because I could not even remember that I had sleepwalked the night before. While sleepwalking, I used to open the door, and I ended up going back to my friend's apartment. Then one day, I ended up going outside, and somebody brought me back to the lobby. My mother was already up looking for me, and she beat me on top of that. It happened for six to eight months after the shooting incident. Later, I went back to live with Helen, who raised me full-time. However, I visited my mother on the weekends. The sleepwalking stopped, and I never experienced it again while living with my godmother for a year.

Eventually, Helen decided she was moving to Newmarket, which was a brand-new place at the time. I remember the backyard only had mud and dirt. She was in transition, and I knew I wouldn't be there for a long time. In due course, I moved back to Jane Street to live with my mother. The sleepwalking restarted, just like the daily crimes I witnessed. After moving back to Jane Street, I went to Jamaica for some time. My mother had her own trauma to work through, so she moved to her mother's house on Jane Street and Grandravine Drive (Down the Lane).

I went to a Catholic middle school for some time. I had just returned from Jamaica, so, of course, I had an accent and spoke fast. And, believe it or not, when I was younger, I used to stutter. The school sent me to therapy to correct the stuttering issue. The Catholic middle school kicked me out because, on Ash Wednesday, I refused to let the preacher grab my face and put ashes on my forehead. The altercation on Ash Wednesday led to my being in the office. The following week was communion. They partnered me with another student named Patrick. He had a Jamaican background, so he understood me more. They wanted me to sit in a box and tell a complete stranger my problems, but I refused to. They forced me to do it, because that was the rule. When I finally went into the box, after being disobedient, the preacher said a couple of Hail Marys, and he asked, "When was your last confession?"

I said, "I don't confess to mankind. If I have a problem, I speak to God, my Father, or my fleshly father."

He shook the gate and repeated the question, "What is your confession?"

I said, "I'm not telling you my fucking problems. Who are you to tell me anything? You're not my Father God, and you're not my fleshly father."

The priest stood up abruptly and stormed out of the box. He grabbed my arm and shook me. I said, "No. Who are you? Don't touch me!" That led to my expulsion from every Catholic school in Toronto.

My mother and my aunt came to the school and said, "Well, you should have explained to us when we registered here that these things would be happening, because she's coming from the Caribbean, and she doesn't know these things. You should have explained it, instead of forcing her into it!" I really did not care at that point, I just wanted to fight him for putting his hands on me.

CHAPTER TWO:

THE FOUNDATION

My maternal grandmother, Gloria, and my godmother, Helen, were best friends. Helen is how Gloria came to Canada. I remember Helen offering Gloria some money to keep me, but Gloria refused. I didn't know why she would refuse her own granddaughter from coming to stay at her place. But I concluded that she just didn't want me at her house. When I travelled back to Canada from Jamaica, I went to live with my mother and grandmother in the Jane and Grandravine area. I already knew a lot of people within that community. It was all because of my father's traction. My father and I used to travel together frequently, so I knew a lot of places and a lot of people. Jane and Grandravine had two parts to it—Bottom Lane and Top Lane. We lived on Bottom Lane. I would play all day, knowing that my dad was in the area—this brought me assurance. I had a few babysitters that would look after me in that area, and I was more present at their houses than I was at my grandmother's house. Sometimes I ended up sleeping at their house.

Once again, I had learned to be an observant person, so when my grandmother expressed her feelings about my living with her to Helen, I knew that there was a problem. I tried to stay out of her way as much as possible. Helen wasn't home all the time, because of the type of work she did, and she didn't like it when I was home alone. She had six kids of her own, but I was the youngest. Gloria and Helen never argued, but one day they had a strong discussion about me. I just walked past them and went to go play. In my grandmother's house were me, my Aunt Pat, and my Uncle Benkey. My Uncle Mark would come by regularly. I was always in and out of the house, because I didn't feel comfortable being there. However, my dad would bring money for my mom and me, or he would buy groceries for the family.

One day during fall, which was back-to-school time, Gloria was cooking Sunday dinner. I came in, and I said, "Evening," to everybody, and she said to me, "No, you should call us by name." I was confused, but I knew she had family over from the United States. Her sister, my Aunt Pat, said out loud, "But she already greeted us. It doesn't need to be that way." I put down my stuff, and then I left. When I came back, I was hungry. At the time, my cousin, Pula, was living with us. She was a chubby child. She was very smart but not street smart at all, as she was sheltered by both her parents and our grandmother. She was very much spoiled and highly favoured by the family. Gloria told me that I had to wait until she was finished eating to eat. I didn't have a problem with it, but I wondered why. At times, I would wait, but eventually I would fall asleep. During the night, my uncle made macaroni and cheese and hot dogs. I awakened to him making it, and he gave me some. This continued to happen, but my mom was not aware that this was going on. However, I was not going to say anything. One day my grandmother said to me, "If you are hungry, then when your cousin is done eating, you should eat off her plate." I immediately reacted by saying, "My dad pays for whatever is cooked in this house." I then slammed the door, and she opened the window to confess what her problem with me was. She then confessed what her problem was with me. I found out that she did not hate me but rather my dad. My grandmother thought that my dad had put her son Jah-Jah on drugs, but that wasn't the case. As she was crying, she admitted that she didn't like me because of what my father did.

I proudly defended my dad. I knew he would never do something like that, because of the many conversations he and I had. He would talk to my uncle, too. I told my grandmother that she had her story wrong, and she was furious. She wanted me to leave her house permanently. She didn't like the idea of me talking back to her, so I left the house. I saw my dad hours later, and I told him everything that was going on in the house. He was enraged. He argued that he was giving money to my family and buying groceries for the house. My mother had moved out prior to this incident and was living with her baby father, so when he came to help deal with the situation, my mother eventually came as well, and he told her she needed to get a place of her own. Aunt Pat interjected and said I could stay in her room. Everyone agreed, but I wasn't allowed to leave the room. I had to stay in the room at all times. Uncle Randy was a good basketball player, and he was coming back from the States at the time that all the drama was happening. I already knew that he had been sent to his mother, from what his dad had told him in the States, but I never said anything, because it wasn't my place. Helen was in her new home, and she was three months in. They were still in the process of building the house. I remember visiting the new place, but nothing was done, not even the backyard or kitchen. Once again, Helen didn't want me to be there, because I was the youngest and I had a tendency to touch everything. I was at my grandmother's for about three or four months. I remember coming home one night, and out of nowhere, my uncle said to me, "I heard what's going on. I'm just telling you; it wasn't your daddy taking the drugs. And your dad told me why he broke up with your mom. Things happen. I don't want you to be like your father."

Uncle Jah-Jah and I share the same birthday. He got me a Cabbage Patch doll. The next morning, I'm not sure if Gloria had overheard us talking, but I came home from school and I couldn't find my Cabbage Patch doll. My uncle bought more items for my doll and offered to buy me a new one. He told me that it was okay. We just sat there and smiled at each other until I fell asleep. Pula, my cousin, admitted that my grandmother had thrown it out, and my uncle and I went into the garbage to look for it. My uncle ended up buying new items for my doll. I spent a lot of time with my babysitter and her children. She was such a nice lady. Everybody knew my dad; therefore, I never went hungry.

Eventually, I lived with Helen at her new place, and then I went to my mother's house. My mother had gotten her own place with her new gentleman, Charles. By this time, she had moved to Rexdale, Jamestown. I lived full-time with my mother, but I visited either my dad or Helen on the weekends. My dad had rivals within Jamestown, so he preferred that I meet him halfway whenever he came to get me. He was living at Falstaff. On Sundays, I would attend The Prayer Palace Church. I used to skip church, because I wanted to spend time with my dad. I would take the Sunday school bus to church, and then ditch to visit my father. I would go to church with my little brother, so I paid him in candy and two dollars to keep quiet. I always tried to rush and make it back on time. Of course, there was one Sunday that I missed the school bus, and the pastor had to bring me home, and, yes, my mother did beat my ass. She was more upset that I had taken my brother out of church and on the journey to see my father. After getting busted, I wasn't allowed to see my father from that time onward. My brother just couldn't keep quiet. By this time, the abuse had increased. I don't know why my mother was so angry with me. Even when I did nothing wrong, I would get the short end of the stick. I don't know what it was.

My mother was pregnant with her fourth child, for her current partner, and they held a lot of parties. My house was the party house back then.

One day, Goldy went grocery shopping, so I took it upon myself to go downstairs, turn on the big sound system, and put on a few records. I turned the music up and scratched away, having the time of my life. Music has always been an outlet for me to escape pain or past traumatic thoughts that crossed my mind. I did not know that my mother was watching me from outside, through the basement window. When she came into the house, she called me and asked me if I had touched the sound system. I lied to her and said, "No. I was playing with my Walkman." I then told her the truth, and I let her know why I touched the sound system and even went into detail as to why I picked the songs I was playing. One of the songs I played was "Can't Touch This" by MC Hammer. I was a part of the upcoming talent show at school. I knew what was coming. My mom brought me to the basement steps and kicked me down the stairs three times. Then she locked the door, and I had to stay down there. I didn't mind, because at least I could be locked off from the world upstairs. The basement was fully furnished, and we had a TV and a fluffy rug. Charles would try to intervene and tell her that she shouldn't be doing this to me. He knew my father and the power that he had. He explained to her that he didn't want to witness the abuse that was occurring. Furthermore, he didn't want me to tell my dad. He would try to save me, but I knew Friday was coming, and I didn't care. Friday was the day for me to escape to my father's place for the weekend.

At that same time, Jamestown had two courts. It was the place that my cousins and I played tag. Classic Burger King was the place to hang out, and Don and I would play outside often. One Wednesday afternoon after middle school, we played. She was at the top of the court, and I was at the other end of the court. While we were playing tag, the game suddenly turned into a water fight. I was soaking wet, and I had a curfew. I had to be home by five o'clock, but that wasn't the case that afternoon. My mom was working nights at the time. She was an intelligent woman but also weird. She was two different women in front of different people. While at work, she talked and carried herself in a different way. When she was around her friends, the Kingstonians, the gangster would kick in. My mother was definitely a smoker, and on Sunday evenings, she would prepare her weed religiously. She would then put them in her flat metallic cigarette case. When I noticed it was six o'clock, I ignored the time and continued to play. Romping was my thing, and I didn't want to leave. Time flew by, and soon it was nine o'clock and people were going home. I decided to go to my cousin's house, because I didn't want to face my mom. I knew what was going to happen. As soon as I got to my cousin's house, her mom looked at me and said, "Your mother is looking for you." My house was two minutes away from the courts, but it took me an hour to get there, because I was pacing. I wanted to get dry, because I didn't want my mom to see me soaking wet. Unfortunately, my pacing didn't work. When I got to the house, she was already at the door, waiting for me. I was focused on going up the steps. Funny enough, my mom didn't beat me that night, but the following morning I was awakened by a whole glass of water. She said, "You want to be wet? Here's wet." She grounded me, and I wasn't allowed outside. After some time, she wanted me to leave the house, but only to go to the store to get batteries for the TV remote. We had a remote control that could be pushed into the TV, and, of course, she thought I had lost it. But it was Jesus, my brother, who had lost it. Nevertheless, I got the blame for it. So, with my smart mouth I said, "Well, but I thought I wasn't allowed outside." I even had a smirk on my face; I was twelve years old at this point. This really upset her. She told me that I was rebellious, and I told her that she was being ridiculous. Later on, she sent me away to my father's place. My mother didn't discipline me; she abused me. I stopped attending school, and at the age of thirteen, I ceased living with my mother. Whenever my mother would beat me, she would say that I had told my father about the drugs. At first, I didn't understand what she was saying to me. I would freeze every time she mentioned the drugs. Then I started to recall what happened in the past. She was angry with her life, and she was never stable again.

CHAPTER THREE:

DEVELOPING WITHOUT MATERIALS

When I lived in Jamaica as a child, my aunt would send me different things from the States, including clothes, shoes, and even snacks. At one point, she sent me a five-pack of Hubba Bubba gum, and each pack of pink gum held five or six pieces. One day, I gave a young boy named Dwayne some of my gum. A week went by, and I noticed that he was still chewing the exact same piece of gum, so I asked him, "Dwayne, how are you still chewing the gum 'til now?" He explained that he thought that was the only piece left, so he tried to preserve it for as long as possible. When I told him I had more, he started to fight with me, asking why I didn't tell him and give him more. It turned out to be a big fight, and he was so upset that he found a stone near my house, and he threw it at me and hit my head. I was tempted to fight him, but I thought at that moment, *"I don't know how to fight a Jamaican!"* When I got home, my aunt was enraged, and she asked what happened. I wasn't trained to lie, but I knew how to twist a story. So, I told her a story about Dwayne and I playing and accidentally getting hurt. A week or so later, I saw Dwayne and the other kids on the road. I invited them to play Duck-Duck-Goose, a popular Canadian game. Usually, I would go outside barefoot, since that was something the Jamaican kids did regularly, although it would piss my aunt off when I would leave the house that way. She didn't want me to conform to some of the kids' ways of doing things, but rather hold true to my Canadian upbringing. But at that time, I didn't care, because on that specific day, I had a plan. I wore my nicest Nike's, and I invited the kids to sit down and play. I then initiated a game of Duck-Duck-Goose. Since it was still quite a new game for everyone, they immediately ran to play with me. When it was my turn, I made sure that when I stood up, I dusted off myself. I was wearing peach shorts and a peach and blue top. As I went around the circle, I gave Dwayne a big slap on his head, and I yelled out, "Goose!" I took off running and never stopped. He was running close behind me, but I couldn't stop, because I knew he would beat my ass. I ran into my aunt's house, ran into her arms, and held her tight, because I was afraid, he would come into the house. She was confused about what was going on, so I confessed that he was the one who had hit my face. Eventually, my aunt and his mom exchanged words.

Later on in life, when I was about twenty-five years old, I went back to Jamaica to visit. I was walking one day, when I heard someone call my name. "Tiny?" I looked at the man, and his face was slightly familiar, although I didn't remember who he was. He said, "It's me,

Dwayne." I pondered for a moment, trying to remember who he was. He then said, "The guy you tried to beat up during the game?"

My guard was immediately up. I said, "Oh, Dwayne, I remember you. How have you been?" We eventually talked about what had happened, and I showed him the scar he had left on my face from hitting me with the stone. He shared with me that he had told his children the story, and had taught them how to play Duck-Duck-Goose as well. At that time, Dwayne introduced me to his girlfriend, but he ended up passing away five or six years after that. He had gotten into an altercation with some guys, and they ended up shooting him. He was on the road to success—he ran his own taxi service. I was happy to know that we got to see each other as adults, and he got to see what he did to my face. He was very apologetic, and he was very remorseful, so rest in peace, Dwayne. I don't get that moment of reconciliation with people often.

In Jamaica, I was treated like a foreign child. They would pay special attention to me, and almost everyone would give me special treatment. But after a while, that treatment stopped. I knew that I wanted to go back home to Canada, because I didn't want the Jamaican life anymore, but my family in Canada didn't want me to come back. I would protest and say, "I'm not Jamaican, and I don't want to live like this any longer." So, when I went to school in Jamaica, it was for a short time, because I would always rebel and stand up for myself. I was not going to be talked down to, even as a child. If an adult was trying to boss me around, I would think to myself, *"Who are you talking to?"* I was in Jamaica for a year. Initially, I had gone there for the Christmas holiday.

Eventually, my passport went missing. My dad had gotten deported to Jamaica during that time as well, so he couldn't bring me back to Canada either. I wasn't speaking with my mother, and my grandmother was working in the States at the time. So, what was I even going back home to? I thought for a moment, *"I might as well stay. It's not like I'm being mistreated here. It's not like I don't know the people here."* As a child, it was tradition that I went to Jamaica for Christmas. So, I went to Jamaica periodically, almost every other holiday, so I was familiar with my community. When I asked my aunt why she would not help me to return to Canada, she said, "When you're in Canada, we hear things, you know. You don't have anybody to guide you, and your dad's not doing the best when it comes to parenting. Yes, he provided some things, but we know what your dad's about, so just stay here."

I told her, "You can't make that choice for me." Ultimately, I made the decision that I was unhappy and wanted to leave. I literally asked around, and a lady named Lynn told me where the Canadian Embassy was. My aunt and Lynn weren't talking at the time, and now Lynn has passed away. I went to the Canadian Embassy, because I thought, *"I'm Canadian. I don't need to be here. I want to send myself back home."* That was how I was able to return to Canada. Still, I'm grateful for growing up in Jamaica, because there were tools and things I learned while I was there that I apply to my everyday life, even now.

When I was thirteen years old, my mother had another child, my sister. She was born prematurely; therefore, she was not able to come home to us right away and had to stay at the hospital for a while after her birth. Soon after, my mother got into a car accident, which led to my taking over the care of my brother, Jesus, which I did not mind at all. On weekends, I would bring him to my godmother's house, and he was able to experience *The Cosby Show* lifestyle that I had always told him about. On weekdays, I lived with my father and his girlfriend, although my brother and I were usually home alone.

One day, my brother and I were home with my mother's new boyfriend, Jeff. He asked me a dumb and uncomfortable question: "Do you have a boyfriend?" He probably asked because I was a tomboy to the core. I would wear my hair in one of two ways: either pigtails or a ponytail. On Sundays, my mother would wash my hair, treat it with mayonnaise, and then press it. Later that day, I would go outside to play with a young man named Sheldon, at the park. One Sunday afternoon, as we were playing, he threw sand in my clean hair. I wasn't happy about it, because my mother was hotheaded, and I knew she would beat my ass. That beautiful evening, I fought Sheldon Bailey like a boy, and I fractured his nose on the playground. I was a fighter back then. We all have a bit of crazy in our childhood.

When Jeff asked me if I had a boyfriend, I said, "Of course, I have a boyfriend, but I am not going to tell you who it is." His next question was, "Does he kiss you and stuff?" I looked at him, and then I asked him, "What are you talking about?" I became uncomfortable to the point of cursing the hell out of him. He called my mom and told her everything that I'd done. She came straight home from the hospital, boiling with anger.

My mother, of course, did not ask me any relevant questions. Straightaway, she shouted, "Why are you trying to break up my relationship?"

As a thirteen-year-old, I quite understood what it felt like to be wrongfully accused. My feelings were hurt, because that truly wasn't the intent of my heart. My response to her was simply, "What are you asking me? Like, are you crazy? No!"

I thought that would have been the end of it, but incidents like that occurred many other times. Jeff would ask me inappropriate questions and, eventually, he started trying to hold one of my hands. The way he held my hand puzzled me. I asked him, "What are you doing?" I took the pen that was on the table, and I stabbed him with it.

He yelled, "I'm going to tell your mom!"

I said, "When you tell her, tell her why you are holding my hand. Choose not to hold my hand and there won't be any problem." I further told him that I was going to tell my dad, and he was very upset about that. Then he put his hand over my mouth and pleaded with me, multiple times, not to tell my dad.

I never told my dad about the incident. Jeff definitely crossed the line, but he didn't do anything to me sexually. I sensed it was going there, though, so I made sure to stop his foolish antics immediately, before things got out of hand. I never told anyone about it; I kept it between Jeff and me. Not that it was a secret, nor was I protecting him. I just chose not to disclose it. One day, my godmother asked me, "What were you and Jeff arguing about?" I didn't go into details with her, I only revealed that he had asked me questions that were inappropriate, and so I stabbed him with a pen. To my surprise, he hadn't told anyone about what I had done to him. My godmother is so Canadianized that it was disrespectful to her to speak in Jamaican patois. I had to communicate with her in standard English. Oh, how I love her!

For six months, I stayed away from my mother's house because of what I had disclosed, and I stayed with my godmother instead. My godmother was very overprotective of me. Since I was not in my mother's home when my sister was born, I didn't get a chance to hold her. At first, I had a limited opportunity to know her, but as time went by, I got to know her. My mother's instinct probably spoke to her, because she eventually ended her relationship with Jeff. Not too long after my mother's failed relationship with Jeff, she introduced me to a gentleman by the name of Paul, from Jamaica. He was a good-looking, clean-shaved, light-skinned man. However, he had no status in Canada, so he needed his permanent resident papers. Keep in mind that my mother was still legally married to my dad, despite the many men connected to her throughout the years.

Paul was a weird person, just like my mother. He wasn't a drug addict, which was a good thing, but he was broke. He didn't see me on weekdays, only on the weekends. I was considered the weekend child, who had the full responsibility of taking care of my brother and sister. Whenever I got to spend time with them, I would take them outside in the evenings, and we would play together. One evening, Paul was prepping for Sunday dinner—it was either a Friday or a Saturday. I believe this is a Caribbean thing. As he cooked in the kitchen, I sat at the dining table, eating pop tarts. The kitchen was enormous, spacious enough for him to do what needed to be done. Paul turned around, looked me straight in the eyes, and said, "You know, for a little girl, you should be doing more in this house whenever you visit us."

I turned to Paul, looked into his eyes, and said, "You can't give me chores! Who are you? What's your name again?"

He got upset and said, "Well, I'm the man of this house."

My response was, "No! This house is Metro Housing, and the man of this house is my brother. Your name is not on any papers here." I knew this because my grandmother told me many things that were happening with, and to, my mother. I continued to say, "You can't put me out when I leave. This house is a three-bedroom, and it can't turn into a two-bedroom. I don't care if you tell my mother! What is she going to do? Beat me? I'm used to that."

Paul was infused with so much anger towards me that he picked up the Dutch pot cover and threw it at me. When he did that, I was like, "What!" He had definitely picked up that behaviour from my mother, and he thought he could abuse me the same way she did. As parents, we must be very careful about the way we treat our children in the presence of others, especially our significant others. Well, his thoughts betrayed him. I wasn't taking it. I started to curse him by the tips of my toes. I cursed him out. When my mother arrived home, I was outside doing my own thing. He told her what had happened between us. I knew deep within me what was coming after. The weekend was ending, and I was getting ready to leave soon to go back to my father's house. That is why I cursed him out so badly—I knew that I wouldn't have to stay at my mom's place much longer. My mother, easily deceived by her partner, asked the neighbour to get me, since I was playing outside. I didn't want to go, to be honest, but I was a child, so I went inside to face the music. I'd be going with my dad soon, I reminded myself.

My mother and Jeff's place was at the end of the tunnel of the Metro Housing complex. When I entered the house, I went into the kitchen and opened the window. I had a strategic plan to make sure that when my dad was coming for me, he would hear the raucous sound from the tunnel. Paul explained the altercation we had, defending himself to my mother, and she immediately dragged me to the corner of the wall. She wanted to defend her stupid man. I noticed that Paul had left out that he had thrown the Dutch-pot cover at me, so I brought it up at that very moment. I said, "He left out the part where he threw the Dutch-pot cover at me, and there's a dent in the wall."

She said, "That's what happened?"

I said, "Ask him how that hole got in the wall."

She turned to him and asked, "Did you throw the pot cover at her?" Paul confessed and admitted what he had done to me. My mother let go of me, and they started to fight. I began to cheer for my mother. I never knew I could cheer for my mother like that. It was the best feeling ever. She beat that man, and I said, "Yes!" At the same time, I was confused, because I was usually the victim, and I had never seen her defend me before. She continued to beat him to a pulp. As I was passing Paul, I kicked him, and it felt so good.

My father came to pick me up from my mother's house, and he asked, "What's going on?" He had witnessed my mother and Paul fighting, and had pulled out his gun. Paul started to plead and explain himself. Knowing me and my prideful self, I said, "No! Ha-ha, he threw the Dutch-pot cover to hit me, and he also said I must wash plates! Remember, I don't live here regularly." My dad turned to him and asked him three times, "Did you give my daughter rules?"

He lied at first, because of the sticky situation he was in, and his nose was already bleeding. I entered the conversation again and said, "No, he's lying! He threw the pot cover at me while he was yelling and screaming." By this time, Helen had taught me not to lie, but sometimes I would exaggerate, so I made the story juicier.

My dad then said, "You're in here beating up on her mom?"

My mom jumped in and said, "No, he wasn't beating up on me."

He made a decision and said to Paul, "Pack up your stuff; you have to leave." My dad helped him pack his little blue suitcase, and put him right out.

When I came back inside, my mom said, "Oh, you mash up my relationship!"

I said, "I what? I fully admitted that he threw the pot cover at me, and you bust his ass. You watched your husband put him out." My mother decided to beat my ass, but I didn't cry. I just took the beating, and that was that. I found out later that when I was not there, Paul was there. My brother told me that Paul still came over. I guess he feared my being there, and that I would tell my dad. Finally, they broke up and she moved to Mississauga.

My mother had a new boyfriend named Kirk, and, of course, she got pregnant again. I felt the need to be a nurturer; therefore, I helped her look after my brothers and sisters. One day, my mom was on her way to work, and she had another accident. It was winter, and the building had five steps to get into it, but they didn't salt the steps, so she ended up falling. She fell down the steps and broke her ankle, to the point where the doctors had to put screws in it. She needed help with the children, because she wasn't family-oriented. Therefore, she left me to care for them. The good thing about me was that I was always ready to help. She promised me that she wouldn't hit me as much as before, but I knew within me that that was a lie. I didn't like when she hit me; nonetheless, I'd rather take the beating myself than let my brothers or sisters endure the pain. There was a time when I travelled to the lake behind our buildings to skate. *The Cosby Show* life showed me how to skate, but my brother didn't know how to ice skate. I still brought him to the lake. He had on a green snowsuit. I said to him, "Come on the lake." Lo and behold, he took one step on the lake, and he sat on it. It wasn't a lot of snow, but it was cold. He sat down and played in the snow. While he played, I was on the lake twirling. Suddenly, I heard the ice cracking. All I could say was, "Oh, my God!" So, I told him not to come on the ice. I tried to run back to him, but the ice gave way. All I could do was look up, and I saw my brother running in the snowsuit back to the building. I tried to catch him, because if he got to that building before me, I was going to get a proper beating. But the ice was giving way. By the time I got out of that water, my brother was long gone. You know, when I got home, I got a proper beating.

My mother said to me, "Oh, you want to come here and act like the dead?"

I said, "I nearly died in the lake. What's the problem? I'm cold and wet, and you're yelling and screaming and carrying on."

My mother did beat me that day. All she could say was, "Suppose you killed my child?"

"But he wasn't even near the lake, though," was my response.

That was her only concern—her Jesus, my brother. I didn't come back to spend a weekend for a while, and when I did come back, my mother had herself another boyfriend, and he was a street guy. He also knew my dad from the streets, so whenever I came over, he was very polite to me. For instance, he would say to me, "Did you do your homework?" At first, I didn't answer, but when my mom used to yell and hit me, he would say to her, "You can't do that. I don't want anyone, including her dad, to think I'm encouraging this behaviour. You know how the streets are run."

My mother was very particular about her home. No matter where she lived, she was always clean. I was fourteen years of age when she decided to make the move. I made it my duty to keep the place neat and tidy, especially for the sake of peace, but knowing the person my mother was, nothing I did was ever good enough. As I was cleaning the house one day, her boyfriend said to me, "If you move the figurine, she will notice." It was a nice evening. My mother came home from work, and she saw a fork in the sink that my brother had left there. She started to curse in Jamaican. She said, "Bumboclot!" I wasn't sure why she was cursing, since I had cleaned up the entire apartment perfectly. Then my brother looked at me and said, "The fork". So, I said, "You didn't wash the fork, really?" Then we both heard her yell, "Kamelah!" She started to curse in Jamaican, again. I went into the kitchen, and I had on my headphones. I was listening to Wu-Tang Clan on my Walkman. She was calling me all types of names, including "bitch," and so in my head, I was calling her names back, not knowing the words were actually coming out of my mouth. She heard me, and when I turned around, I saw her.

I saw her lips moving, but I couldn't hear what she was saying, because the music volume was too high. I watched her as she picked up the brass stand and wacked me across my forehead with it. That's all I remember. When I woke up, I felt really warm. I still have the scar today. She gave me a gash straight across my face. Her boyfriend said to her, "She needs to go to a hospital."

She just called him crazy, saying they would take the other kids away. She didn't want me to go to Helen's, she didn't want me to go to my dad's, and she didn't make me go to school. They just dressed the wound for a short time.

When I ended up going to my godmother's house, she asked, "How did you get that cut on your face?" I told her about the lake story, and she said, "Okay. Did you go to the doctor?" And I said, "No." So she ended up bringing me to a doctor.

The doctor said, "I don't know who puts Vaseline and iodine on this, but you need stitches." So, I got stitches that same day.

When my dad saw me, he asked, "How did you get that cut?" And I told him the truth. He said, "Why didn't you tell Helen the truth?"
I said, "Well, I did tell her the truth about the lake, but I just didn't tell her about the other story, because it was in the same timeframe. I knew what the outcome would be, and I didn't want my brothers and sisters to be taken away from the family and end up in the system. So, I told a half-truth."

My dad went to my mother's house and said, "Enough is enough! She's not coming back here, because the hit you gave her cracked her skull." The X-ray showed that that was the case. So that was it. I was sad, because I wouldn't be seeing my brothers and my sisters, although they sometimes called me. She ended up having a son for that boyfriend, and they moved back to Jane and Finch. I was in high school when she made the decision to relocate there. They moved to the heart of Jane and Finch, close to my high school. I started to see my brothers and sisters regularly, and I saw my mom basically every day in the mall. She would stop to see a friend in the mall after work. Her friend had a restaurant, and I would pass through there with my friend. Sometimes I didn't say hi, and sometimes I did. Unfortunately, by this time, my father had been deported. I never told anyone. She got word of it, though, and said, "Well, come stay with me." At the time, I was travelling from Newmarket to go to school. It was a long journey back and forth, and it was becoming hectic. So, I took her up on her offer. She was hardly home, so I ended up watching the children. To be honest, the physical abuse stopped, and it was now just verbal abuse. Her primary focus was work and then hanging out with her friends. Then she started travelling a lot. I was home alone with the kids. One of the trips was longer than usual. She left, and then she never came home. She was usually away for a week or two weeks, but now it had been a month. My dad wasn't in the country at the time, as he had gone to the United States.

I was getting the kids ready, dropping them to daycare, and attending school myself. The daycare teacher suspected something wasn't right, and one day decided to follow me home, after I picked up the kids. I thought she was just nosy, but maybe she was just concerned. She knocked on the door, and I opened it for her. She asked, "Where's your mom?"

I said, "She's at work."

She said, "No problem. I'm going to sit here until she returns."

I said, "Okay. Well, do you want a glass of water?"

I thought to myself, *"What am I going to do?"* Suddenly, I remembered my god-sister. I always thought she was really cool. Even though they lived in Newmarket, she worked in Toronto. So, I went into the bathroom and called her. "I can't find my mom. She's not home, and the teacher is sitting here and she wants to talk to an adult." I explained everything to my god-sister on the phone. She was at work and was able to leave, so she said she'd be there in half-an-hour. When I hung up, I turned to the daycare teacher and said, "Okay, she'll be here in an hour. She's at work." Lo and behold, she came in twenty minutes, only to be met with the teacher's demands to see my mother.

"Her mother is doing a double shift, so I'm here to stay with them." She was working at some office, and she pulled out a badge to show the teacher. They had a short conversation, and then the teacher left. My god-sister didn't know I was home alone regularly with my younger siblings, and she inquired about my mother's whereabouts. "Ok, what's going on?" she asked.

I had no answer to give. Days later, we found out that my mother was in jail for importing drugs. My godmother and her friend went to bail her out. That was another milestone for me.

When my mother came home, she said, "You actually held out?"

I said, "It was like a month. Where were you for a month? You left me with your three children to deal with, and I'm a child. I have things to do. I don't have time for this. Even the teacher followed me home."

I knew that she had money in her room whenever she went away, but I didn't want to touch it. My dad's girlfriend at the time gave me lunch money anyway, so that's what we were surviving off of. And anytime my mother travelled, she would do a proper grocery shopping first, so there were groceries still in the house. I would cook for the kids and make sure they were fed.

When she came out of prison, she reasoned with me. She told me, "Well, I don't want you to look down on me, but this is something I've been doing for years." She took the time to explain it to me. The conversation was over an hour long, and it was very detailed. It was as if she was educating me on the streets. I already knew both my parents were from the streets, but my godmother didn't want me in that type of environment. She said to my mother, "You need to figure out what to do with the kids, and call their father to sort things out, because you have these charges against you, and you could get a lot of jail time." Afterwards, my mother began to think about what her next steps would be.

CHAPTER FOUR:

INSTABILITY BEFORE THE FALL

My mother ended up moving to St. Clair West for some time. I guess the police knew her address, because it didn't take her long before she relocated to the heart of Jane and Finch. She changed her addresses frequently, maybe it was because of her street life. On the eve of my birthday, September 16th, my mother asked me if I could watch the kids for her. I agreed to it; however, I expressed to her that I already had big plans with my friends. We were planning on going to the movies, getting something to eat, going downtown, and shopping at the Eaton Centre. I also had a seven o'clock appointment to get my hair done—nothing extravagant, I just wanted my hair to be washed, treated, and pressed. I was going out with my friends, so I had to present myself well, and on top of that, it was in the downtown area where all the upper-class people either lived or went to hang out. Even though my dad wasn't in the country, he still used to pay my hairdresser bill. My father was so well known that he had connections everywhere. He was friends with the owner of a sneakers store in the Jane and Finch

Mall. It was a drug-related friendship. Every week, I got a new pair of sneakers, plus I got to do my hair, because my dad would pay them in advance for whatever shoe or style I wanted. Even though I didn't do my hair often, as I was never that girly, I didn't like to comb my hair myself. I couldn't manage all of my hair. Whenever I didn't use my credits at the shoe store or hairdresser, my friends would utilize it. There was a restaurant in the mall, and my dad, or his friends, would pay the owner one hundred dollars a week, so I could go there and get what I wanted.

My mother wasn't the most loving towards me; however, I didn't mind watching the children for her so she could go about her business, as long as she came back on time. That afternoon, I decided to watch the kids from the hallway. I opened the door, and used the telephone book to prop the apartment door open. I never actually went into her apartment. It's not that I was not welcome in the apartment, but I just had my own plan for that day. I instructed them on what to do. I would tell them to go and have a bath, and then they came to the door with the lotion and Vaseline for me to lotion their skin. Afterwards, I helped them with their homework at the door. I stayed on the hallway carpet the whole time. I paged my friend to get them Happy Meals from McDonald's.

It was seven o'clock, and I was still babysitting when I should have been out with my friends. When I saw that it was eight o'clock, I thought to myself, *"The time to hang out with my friends has passed, and my hair is still in a mess."* I said to the kids, "Okay, go into your rooms and lay down. I'm going to stay right here at the door until she comes." The superintendent of the building cleaned at night. He had his mop and vacuum in his hands, ready to work. He kindly asked me to go into the unit so he could do his job. "Damn it," I said to myself. So, I ended up going into the apartment. The telephone book was still holding the door open while he was cleaning. I stood right at the door and, eventually, I got tired of standing. I went back and forth in my mind about whether to get a dining chair to sit on. I knew my mother to the core, and I didn't want her to come and say that I had done anything to her apartment or that her place was dirty. I wanted to avoid doing the little things that triggered her. I wanted her to come home and see her place the same way it was before I got there. The children woke up, and our mother was still not home. I instructed them to stay with me by the door, because I didn't want them to touch anything. I went and threw the garbage from the Happy Meals into the garbage chute, so there were no problems when she came home. The old man was almost finished cleaning, when my mother and her friend came out of the elevator. They had their bags and boxes in their hands. I stood there and watched them struggle as they walked towards the unit. I was ready to leave.

She was mad that her door was open and asked if someone was there. I said to her, "Listen, let me tell you something: I wasn't even in the unit for twenty minutes. I've been in the hallway the whole time."

This woke my brother up, and he confirmed to her, "No, we were inside. She was in the hallway."

My mother asked, "They weren't in the hallway?"

We all said, "No," at the same time. I told them to go back to bed and that I would see them soon.

I said to her, "They ate McDonald's, they bathed, and they did their homework. I'm leaving." I didn't ask her any questions as to why she stayed so long.

She pushed me against the wall and said, "Oh, I have to check the house first."

I laughed and replied, "You can do whatever you want. I'm leaving."
The mop was close to her, by the kitchen, and while I was passing, she hit me with it. I grabbed the mop stick from her. "You can't hit me again; I'm not a kid. What are you doing? I just want to leave."

Her friend said, "You know she didn't do anything if she watched the kids from the hallway. She must have a reason why she did that."
I said to her friend, "You see how she's behaving? This is the reason I did that."

She pushed back to get the mop stick away from me, and I let it go. Oh, she created a scene. She was claiming that I hit her with the mop stick, but her friend saw exactly what had taken place, and knew that what my mother uttered wasn't the truth. She tried to hit me one more time, as I made my way to the door. Then she barricaded the door and called the police. I did not move until they got there. She told the police that I hit her. So, I said, "Could you call my godmother? I have no clue what she's talking about. Could you please just call this number, and speak with her?"

The officer said with authority, "Well, the parent is saying that her child is abusing her. What do you want us to believe?" What he said confirmed what I already knew—he didn't believe me.
I said, "I don't even live here."

The officer asked me, "What are you doing here?"

"Oh my gosh, she asked me to babysit the kids. I babysat the kids from the hallway." The officer was confused. He asked, "Why would you do that?"

I explained that she was very particular about the way her house was kept. Then I said, "I don't have the time for this. Can I just go, immediately?"

My mother put on a piece of *Days of Our Lives* acting, as if she was this concerned parent, and implied that something might be wrong with me. Her friend had left when she called the police. The police officer asked if any witnesses were there. I told them that the kids could tell them. My brother came and wanted to speak up. However, my mother shoved him away and directed him into the room. They called my brother again, and he said to the officer, pointing, "I sat right there and ate my McDonald's, and she helped us with some colouring and stuff."

The police asked him what happened after, but he didn't have an answer to that.

They went aside and had a conversation, but by the way the officer looked at me, I knew he sided with her and believed her over me. I was later transported to Covenant House. Covenant House is a youth shelter. I didn't know Helen's number by heart, and they took my pager and my phone book away. I looked it up in the general phone book, but it was not listed. Afterwards, I remembered the bakery that was close to where my godmother lived. The baker and Helen were close friends. I looked up the bakery's number, got in touch with that specific baker, and filled her in on what was taking place. My godmother and my father's girlfriend came to the youth shelter, and his girlfriend signed for me to be released. I was out of there in less than a week. That was the good part; the sad part was I turned sixteen in custody. I don't know how they got word that I was there, but I was called to the office, and I saw my dad's girlfriend and Helen. My dad's girlfriend signed me out, not my godmother. I don't know why, and I did not ask. The incident with my mother happened around ten o'clock, and by the time I got to the station, it was after midnight. After I got out of custody, my godmother, my dad's girlfriend, and I went to get something to eat at Harvey's. While at Harvey's, Helen said, "Well, your mom was wrong for what she did. I know you did not do the things she said. However, your money is on its way."

I was like, "Huh? What?" I didn't remember anything about any money. A few minutes later, it all made sense. It brought me back to the time I stayed with my aunt in New York when I was younger. She had entered me in a baby pageant contest. However, I wasn't able to access the prize money until I was sixteen.

My mother remembered that, and she thought my saying that I had things to do meant that I was going to spend all the money on my friends and buy foolishness. So, knowing I was going to get the money the next day, she intentionally called the police to prevent that from happening. I didn't even remember anything about the money. It was far from my mind, because I never lacked anything. My stepmother at the time had three kids for my dad. She used to take care of me. She bought me nice clothes, brought me to get my hair done, and provided food for me to eat. She had a lot of friends from the streets, so whenever I got clothes from her, it was usually a lot. And I was allowed to wear her clothes, even though I had my own. So, I didn't need that money. I never dwelt on it. Once I left Covenant House, I stopped talking to my mother. What she had done didn't make sense to me. But I never let that get in my way, because it had already happened, and there was absolutely nothing I could do about it.

My mother and I couldn't get along, no matter how hard I tried to please her. I was overjoyed when I got news that my dad was coming back to Canada. As I mentioned before, he had gotten deported by the police because of the life he was living. This occurred numerous times. I thought my dad would have never stepped foot on these grounds again, but he did. As soon as he arrived, he rented us an apartment at Jane and Wilson. It was a little building—three stories, no elevator. I was still in high school at the time. I used to go to his baby mother's house close by; he had also rented an apartment over there for her. It so happened that her three kids ended up staying with us for a while, because she was caught by the police and was imprisoned. So, I had to take on the role of their mother and care for them. Upon her release from prison, she came to live with my dad, me, and her kids, but for some reason, we didn't get along. I can recall the physical fight we had over my en suite. Her plan was to take over my bedroom, because it was big and had an en suite. My anger towards her consumed me, and I said to her, without fear, "This is my room!"

She replied, "Oh, but you are a child."

I responded, "I cannot live here any longer. I have had enough of you!

You do not appreciate the fact that I have watched and cared for your children for six months while you were behind bars." My dad overheard what was transpiring between us, and yes, my dad sided with me. After all, I am his first child, whom he loves dearly. He said to her, "You know what? She's been taking care of the kids. I'm in the streets, and I don't have time for that. She's been here with the kids most of the time."

You would think that my dad had learned his lessons by now, but he hadn't. He was still on the streets, doing his transactions. This woman my dad was with didn't want me to have company over. She created a lot of rules that I wasn't used to. Deep within me, my instinct said, *"I can no longer live here."* I needed my own space and peace and quiet. So, I said, "You know what? Here's what is going to happen. You guys can keep this apartment, and I'll move back to the old apartment."

He said, "Okay, but that's not going to happen today."

I said, "Well, I will go to my godmother." My godmother's house was always open to me, and I had my own room.

The words that I spoke pierced my father's heart. He wasn't going to lose his daughter over someone who disliked her, in this case his baby mother. As time went by, it was just me and my dad once more in the apartment, and he kept running the streets and living his life. We hardly had time for each other; he was too busy doing his thing. I mostly heard his voice when he called or came in late.

You may ask, "So where is your mother in all of this?" The truth is, there still wasn't any form of communication between us. However, my siblings weighed heavily on my mind. I missed seeing them and getting them sneakers ever so often, because I had the sneaker connection. If I did get my brothers and sisters sneakers, I would drop it off at their daycare for them. That was the only way to see them. My dad eventually got the apartment back for us. It was empty at the time, but my dad always got groceries.

I remember coming in from basketball one day to find no dinner, no call, no lunch money. It was the same thing the next day and the day after that. That was not like my dad at all. He never came home. A week later, he passed a message with somebody, saying he was in jail. I didn't know what I was going to do. I had this empty apartment, and all I had was clothes. Since his baby mother and I had argued, she stopped giving me clothes. One thing about me is that I never gave up on school. So, my bed for the time was my clothes. I got up every morning, brushed my teeth, washed my face, and got ready. The only thing I ate was boiled eggs, macaroni and cheese, and noodles. The groceries ran out, and my dad's friends that were normally there for me were either disappearing for a period, dead, deported, or in jail. I could've gone back to my godmother's house, but I did not want her to question me about my dad. He had one or two friends. They used to check up on me, but they thought I was at the other apartment. They didn't know that I had moved. I saw one of them one time at the mall, and he gave me two hundred dollars. I used the two hundred dollars to get some groceries and buy stuff for myself. I didn't want to feel left out when I was out with my friends.

I had a best friend named Tyson. She lived at Jane and Finch, and I liked to go to her house a lot. Sometimes I would even sleepover on the weekends, because I didn't want her mom to ask me about my dad. Everybody knew my mom and I didn't get along, so they didn't ask me about her much. I would go by Tyson's house after school, and by seven o'clock I would go home. Little did they know that I was going home to an empty apartment. I had no TV, and there was no internet in those days, so it was just me, my thoughts, my clothes, and my homework. That lasted for two months. During that time, a white man would knock on the door, but I never answered it. He came back religiously, sometimes two times a day. And one day he said, "Well, I know somebody is here," and he pushed a Leon's Furniture card under the door. It said, "Call me." I never did. I also didn't turn it over until that weekend when I was cleaning up. It was a Leon's card. I guess it was one of my dad's clients. Then I remembered seeing a letter from Leon's. The man wrote me a long note, but I never paid attention to flyers that people pushed under the door; I would just push them to the side or throw them away. One day, the note said, "Well, I know your dad is not here, and I had made a promise to him. I was here to furnish the apartment, but you refused to open the door. So please give me a time. I can drop it off." After that, I started to open up all the other letters. He'd been writing to me and wanting to bring the furniture for about a month.

I took the bus and went to the store. I gave the card to a lady at the front desk. She said, "Well, he's not in today. He will be here tomorrow."

I said, "Okay, could you have him call me?" I gave her my phone number, and he ended up calling me the next morning.

He said, "Tiny,"—only somebody who knew my dad would call me Tiny, because, at the time, I had outgrown that name.

I said, "Yes."

He said, "You got my letter, finally. Are you okay?"

I said, "Yes."
"Oh, can I stop by today and give you some money?" he asked.

I said, "I'm fine."

He said, "Okay, well, I'm going to stop by on Wednesday and deliver some of the furniture. What size bed do you want?"

At the time, I didn't know how to size a bed, so I just said, "A bed."
"Do you want a big bed?"

I remembered that my mom always had a big bed, and I was afraid of it, because it was so big. I said, "No, I don't like the big beds." I didn't know it was called a king-sized bed at the time.

"Okay then, I can get you a queen."

I said, "I am a queen, so that's what I deserve."

Lo and behold, he did come. He brought me a lovely black leather reclining sofa, carpet, a coffee table, end tables, a TV, a dining table, and a microwave stand. He also brought me a full bedroom set. It couldn't even fit in the room. I ended up putting one of the night stands by the dining table. I was eternally grateful to God for providing. Nobody knew what I was going through at the time, because I acted normal. God came through for me. I had a fully furnished apartment. I danced that evening. Yes, I danced. I danced. I danced until I fell asleep. But funny enough, I never slept on the bed. I still slept on the floor, for a few days; there was now a carpet, though. A week or two later, I started to sleep on the sofa, and then I began to sleep on the bed. However, I was still home alone, and somewhat low on money.

CHAPTER FIVE:

THE ENGINEERS

A brand-new school year was about to begin. My birthday was around the corner, and I was turning seventeen years of age. My dad had returned, and he was so proud of me for managing things on my own. He said, "I'm so proud of you. You kept yourself out of trouble." Then he handed me some money.

I responded, "If you ever knew how many days I would hate coming here."

"So what time is your friend coming?" he asked.

"No, no one comes here. I was here by myself the whole time. I went to school and still obtained good grades, and I was home by eight o'clock on weekdays. The furniture arrived late, because I did not open the door to your friend." It was just the way of the streets. I wouldn't open the door to this white man that I didn't know, not at my primary location.

We eventually moved in with his girlfriend, and that apartment became a base for his friends. A few months passed, and he ended up being wanted again by the police. I said to myself, *"This is getting out of hand now."*

The police would harass me, and I didn't want to experience that again. My godmother brought me to a place downtown to take off his last name, and I got my mother's maiden name, Blair. Helen thought that the harassment would slow down or stop, but the police knew who I was. They would come to my high school and my hang-out places, when they couldn't find my dad. It became a bit much after a while, so I started to build resentment towards my dad, again. I didn't want my dad's troubles. His troubles were my troubles, but I was only just his child; I was not his actions. Moreover, I'm a girl. Their main problem was that I knew more than I would tell them. I told them absolutely nothing, in fact. Whenever they questioned me about his whereabouts, I would tell them, "When you find him, you let me know. I haven't seen him for years, or months, and I want the child support he owes my mother." That was my line that I said to them every time.

I used to be out with my dad in the streets at nights with his friends. I would help the group rob people. While being raised by my godmother, I was in a Girl Guides group. I hardly went door-to-door selling cookies. My dad and his friends would just buy the boxes. I utilized my Girl Guides uniform to knock on people's doors and say that I'm lost. Someone would open the door, and the group would rob them. That was my job at night. I learned how to drive by participating in this activity, which started at the age of fourteen. We didn't do it every night, but at least once a week. If not once a week, then my dad would bring me on his home invasions every other week. His friends would ask if I could come with them, wearing the Girls Guide uniform, but the look I used to give them never needed an answer.

I had a gold chain with two solid gold dice, and the numbers were diamonds. I wore that chain daily, to the point where my friend called me Jax. I would walk through the mall after school, wearing the chain and dressed like a tomboy. I always had on a tracksuit, either Adidas, Nike, Phat Farm, or Puma. I used to roll up one pant leg, like a little boy, and I always had on the latest sneakers. By this time, I had stopped doing pigtails, because pigtails were too childish. I only wore my hair to the side or the back in a ponytail. One particular day, I had on the Eagles jacket, a black and green Nike tracksuit, and a pair of Scottie Pippen Nikes. Back in the day, every week, girls would meet up with fights. I only lost two fights in my life. I could fight. I was also a mouthpiece, and because I could speak Jamaican more than the regular Canadian, I could curse you out and make you want to fight me. I tore down that mall regularly, and ate at McDonald's repeatedly. I think I was banned from the mall every week, and I was still back, but the people knew my dad, so they couldn't really ban me.

In those days, the big stores in the mall were Woolco and BiWay. *One day, as I was* coming around the corner, where the restaurant was, my mom was there drinking soup on the right side of the restaurant. I stopped and asked the chef, "What's on the menu?" from the left side of the restaurant. He gave me a list of dishes, and I picked fried chicken, rice and peas, salad, and gravy on the side. I went to a sneaker store to see what was new, while I waited on my food. As I entered, he said, "I've got new stuff. You're going to love it," and he pinched my cheeks. He showed me six pairs, and I wanted all six. "I'll pick it up Friday," I said.

"Oh, Bella," he said, "I know. They will be waiting for you."

My best friend, Tyson, and I used to dress the same. I would get my sneakers for free, and she got hers for half price. A few times, I got her free ones. I was so excited to let her know about the new sneakers he had shown me. While walking back into the restaurant, I was thinking about which tracksuit I was going to buy. There was an upcoming rap battle talent show in two weeks, and a few of my friends were entering. The chef passed me my food, and I thanked him. A strong gentleman was sitting there, staring at me. I could see him from the corner of my eye, and I could most definitely feel him staring at me. I ordered patties from the other side of the restaurant. *At that other part, there were* three or four benches, where you could sit and dine in at the counter— that's where my mom was sitting down. I said, "Hello."

She said, "Afternoon, Miss," in return.

While the man was sitting on the corner, I could see him from my right.

"Hey, little girl, where you get that chain from?"

I didn't answer him. He asked again, but this time his voice got a bit louder. He turned his head to the corner, so we were looking at each other. "Hey, you mi ah talk to, you nuh hear mi? Where you get that chain from? Answer me."

I looked him straight in his tough face and said, "You can't ask me that. Who are you? You're rude and bright!" By this time, my mom put down her soup cup so hard I could hear it.

The man proceeded to get up, and he draped me up and slapped me in the face, and then he broke the chain from around my neck. I looked in his face, and I remembered him. I just did not know from where. I was more focused on the slap I had just received. I have sensitive skin, so I could feel his handprint on my face.

Goldy jumped up and threw the remainder of the soup at him. My mom, my friend that was passing by at the time, and I fought the man in the mall. We fought him to the point where he was asking us to stop. The chef tried to part the fight, but that did not work. I don't know who told my dad's friends, but they ended up coming to the mall. There was a door close to where we were. They came full force and pulled him out through the side door.

There was a huge excitement in the Jane and Finch mall, even the police ended up coming by this time, and we ended up leaving. When my dad saw my face, he was so upset. My mom called my dad and said, "You have her wearing the stuff you take from people. This could have been worse, and suppose I wasn't there?" They went at it for a while. My dad asked her if she was hurt and if she was okay, over and over. He said "Sorry," multiple times. The man was big, though, like the Incredible Hulk, and he had slapped me back into 1982. Even later that evening my ears were still ringing. My dad went to see Godly, to make sure she was okay, and I went along for the ride and to get food. I could hear my mom saying, "You can't have her outside doing things. She's a girl; she's not a little boy. You cannot have her outside doing certain things. I didn't do the best job. I brought her into this world, and I'm not going to let your lifestyle take her out. She's not with me, but you're not doing any better. You should be proud she's not like us. She doesn't even smoke." She was right, and she was calm. I don't drink to this day. I have never smoked, and I have never touched my dad or my mom's weed.

She sat down and told him, "I can't give her what you and Helen give her, because she has everything." I could tell she felt bad.

My mom never physically gave me money. My mom used to buy me one or two things, but she didn't need to, because, as I said, my dad's baby mother took care of me, so I always had clothes. My aunts in New York used to send me stuff, and my grandmother used to buy me clothes. But I couldn't wear tight clothes, even though I used to wear jogging suits. She didn't like that when I went to Helen's, I had to wear blouses, button-up shirts, cardigans, jeans, and stuff. So, I always had two styles of dressing, because I lived two different lives. right?

"You can't turn her into something that you know to be wrong," my mom said. Godly wasn't the first person to tell him that; his baby mother and Helen told him as well. My mother was upset with my dad after that situation, and she went on and on. "You can't have her up and down at the base, because she's hearing what's going on. You can't have her as the getaway driver." To this day, I drive with two feet—one foot on the brake and one on the gas. That's how I learned to drive. My mom was schooling him and saying, "You can't have Kamelah out here doing your dirty work. People know her, and she goes places on her own. She's popular, you're famous, and I'm popular. Look what just happened. It could have been worse; not because she's your child doesn't mean she's untouchable. She's a girl. You have to try to raise her as a girl. Stop treating her like she's your son." She went to pick up the phone to call Helen, and the three of them got into an argument.

"Well, that was your job. You're supposed to raise her as a daughter. And, you know, you didn't do that. This is all I know— the streets," my dad said.

It was unbelievable to hear Goldy spitting facts while I was in the kitchen, still eating slowly and thinking, *"Who told her so much stuff, in such great detail?"*

My dad did put us in the streets, but he made sure at nighttime that we still read our Bible, and then he would let me jump on the bed. I didn't know what it meant until I got older, and he taught me that my body and mind need exercise before I fall asleep. We used to read the Bible first; wherever it dropped open, we just read it together. He then said, "Jump on the bed, Tiny. Jump, jump, jump." As a child, I looked forward to nighttime jumping and reading with my dad. Funny enough, my Uncle Jah-Jan used to let me do the same thing.

My uncle had passed away around this time. He loved me unconditionally. His passing put a damper on my spirit, because when my dad was in and out of the country, if I couldn't find my dad, I could always find my uncle. My Uncle Jah-Jah was a blind man. He wasn't born blind; he became blind one night at a party. Jah-Jah was a Rastafarian, and he was also in the streets. He was the only blind man to rob a bank. A lot of people thought his going blind would stop him from being a real "O.G." However, even though he was blind, he was respected. He loved me so much more because we were born on the same day. There was nothing I asked for that I couldn't get from him. My dad never told me "no." I was never wrong with my dad. I have never been with my uncle. With my godmother, I knew how to get things. If I cried, that was it. "Who troubles Tiny?" She never wanted me to be upset when I was in her presence. I think that's how I learned how to be a con artist. I knew how to get around when I wanted something.

At the time of his passing, I was staying with him downtown, on Dupont, the same time as the altercation in the mall. When he heard what happened, he told me about the new world, which is precisely what we're living in today. He didn't use the word "bitcoin," but he explained it. He described the new world for me. He said, "Tiny, I know that we're not the best example, but you have to do better than what we're doing. I don't know if he knew he was going to pass, but that same week, every day I came home, he sat me down and talked to me. "You're not a boy. You're not a girl. You're not a gangster. You cannot be what we are. You need to break the cycle somewhere, and you need to be the one to break the cycle, because your aunts are terrible." Yes, his sisters could curse you out in five minutes. My great-grandparents were hardcore. However, my grandmother was very humble. My grandmother Lynnette was very soft-spoken. She was a very serious business woman, noted in her community, and she loved to travel. Whenever I was in Jamaica, we would sit and have conversations about absolutely nothing. She allowed me to dress girly all the time, because she hated to see me in jeans. When I was home, she made it a point of duty to call me every Sunday after church. Sometimes we just sat there and said nothing. I would ask her, "Are you falling asleep?" And she would say, "No," even though I could hear her snoring. She would feel me and what's going on in the community, and she would let me know that she was travelling out to the country or going up to the big house, where my aunt resided. She always asked me when I was coming back. My grandfather was a gangster. I didn't meet my grandfather, but I had visions of him. When I would share my dreams, they would say, "That's your grandfather."

Even though my dad and Uncle Jah-Jah were doing bad things on the streets, we used to go to church each Sunday, an Orthodox church. I never understood it, because the men stood on one side and the women on the other. You had to take off your shoes and wrap your hair, and they did not speak English most of the time, so I couldn't understand it. My uncle used to explain stuff to me during the two weeks, every day when I came in. My uncle made sure he was home after school, and he used to cook. The food was delicious, even though he was a vegetarian. He said, "Tiny, you're brilliant. You're going to school and getting good marks. Please finish school. Sometimes you have to tell your dad 'no;' don't just agree with what he asks of you. I know that you're trying to be obedient, but don't be disobedient to your path." I didn't understand at that moment, but when he passed, everything he said to me in that two-week period came to light, and at that time, I also found out that I was pregnant.

Uncle Jah-Jah was a tall, heavy-set man, and he was wise. He spoke in quotes. It was never a conversation; it was always wisdom, quotes from the Bible, and quotes from history, but I knew he had an angry side that he never showed to me. I only heard of it. The day of his passing, he got sick. He was in the hospital, and even though he was blind, he was very racist. He was a true Rastafarian, so he still carried that burden of slavery. He took that burden with him. He was talking about Malcolm x and, again, wisdom stuff in the hospital. They ended up calling me at school, because he wouldn't listen. He listened to me, even though I was the little one. He looked at me, and I said to him that day, "What is it that you don't want her to do?"

"This white bitch! She's yelling at me, and she doesn't want me to talk. They're drugging me, and they don't want me to talk." He was speaking wisdom, Bible verses, and slavery stories to them, and they didn't want to hear that. So, my Uncle Jah-Jah passed away from an overdose, because they ended up putting too many drugs in his body. Because of what he said to me in his passing, I knew that I had to change the mindset that I had, or at least try to.

When he would speak, I would listen and say, "You're talking gibberish." But I'm thankful for it, because I've lived to see every gibberish thing come to pass, literally. I knew of the technology that was coming. I knew that there would be no money. I knew that a lot of ungodly things were coming. I knew people would stop being loving. I knew a lot, because my uncle would sit me down and tell me what was coming. "This is what you need to do. You need to prepare yourself," he said. He knew whenever I brought friends over, because he explained that when you lose one sense, another sense gets stronger. He would say, "I know you had a bad day. Smile, Tiny, or sing a song or remix a song, just to make me laugh." He was a very wise man, who would go above and beyond for me, even though he had two children of his own.

CHAPTER SIX:

WISDOM BUILDS A HOUSE

Uncle Jah-Jah was older than my dad. My dad was the youngest. Uncle was a family-oriented man with two children and a wife. He was a graduate of Architectural Drafting and Business Finance from Jamaica. He came to Canada in the late 1970s. He liked to cook, and he also liked to hang out in the community, preferably in a group setting, where he would be able to teach words of wisdom to the street from the Bible. He religiously sang Psalm 91 all the time, with his rhythm, just so people would remember it.

He became blind because of an incident at a club he attended with my parents and a handful of friends. They were all well-dressed when they participated in this party, wearing three-piece suits, furs, and Kangol hats. Somebody at the event had an issue with a group that was in attendance, and a shooting occurred in less than an hour. There were rounds of gunplay, but nobody passed away. However, a lot of people got injured. During the shooting, a large number of beer bottles shattered, and a piece of glass got into my uncle's eye, which blinded him. He was also shot in his shoulder, and this incident took a toll on him, resulting in his not being able to perform his duties as an architect. In turn, it affected his finances, and his life as a whole. Although he lost his sight, he could still help others in his field of work. However, he was no longer wanted, so all he could do was go back to a life of crime. Even though he was crying "Peace" to a few, he went back to that life, because people looked up to him. He was a father figure in the streets. He was well respected. My uncle also didn't want anything to happen to his brother, which was another reason why he chose to involve himself. He would say, "I'd rather be with you than without you."

My uncle's disabilities did not stop him from doing anything. He would do a robbery or two just to maintain his reputation. My uncle and father had a close bond. When they both came around, the combination was strong. During that time, a lot of my dad's friends were moving to Canada from Jamaica, so my uncle started to detach himself from my dad. His mindset was, "You're not alone, and I would rather be wise than be a man who is just known for a crime."

He would sit me down to speak with me, and he would say, "Tiny, now I know you see what's going on. You cannot teach the next generation what you don't see. I'm letting you know to use the knowledge that I have taken from the streets and apply it to Wall Street. What they teach you in school is what they want you to know. I'm teaching you what you need to know."

As I got older, and as the world changed, these remained lessons that I can pass on to my children, nieces, nephews, friends, and family members. I can also apply the old wisdom to this new world. His passing made me sad, but more so frustrated, because I wanted more knowledge. There were so many puzzles that were not complete, quotes and stories that were not complete, because my next daily lesson did not come. However, I got the answers and learned so much from his funeral. The bishop and others spoke highly of him. When people spoke, and they gave their stories, they said things that he had never told me before. It was as though he was speaking through them to connect with me. There were over twenty people that spoke at my uncle's funeral. The funeral was so powerful that we told the funeral director to give us more time. The director turned and said, "Wow, this was an amazing man." He was also gaining knowledge as everybody else was. They weren't sad. It was lesson after lesson about things that he had said to them, either in passing or while hanging out. I got the answers to the puzzle from the funeral. I was truly grateful. My uncle also taught me how to solve problems. Even when he helped me with my homework, he used to sing it to me in a lullaby. For example, he would sing, "Mary had a little lamb." His singing of the answers was a mechanism for me to remember. Now I know that even when the work gets hard and frustration kicks in, I should try to make it fun by singing a song and being glad in it. These are things that he instilled in me as a child, as part of the playground.

He would also say, "Consider your friends. You should be able to tell a true friend how you feel, and walk away. But, of course, some people you call friends may just consider you an associate and will want it to get physical. Use your words and be loud. Let your voice be powerful. Don't fight with your words. Say what's on your mind." I explained to him that sometimes my words got me in trouble and made people want to hit me. I probably told them about their mother and auntie, or facts about themselves and their families, which led to a fight because of my words. I did not have to hit you; I could uppercut you with my words, and I could send you to bed with words. I had absolutely no filter. Overall, Jah-Jah spoiled me. The only time I've heard my dad and my uncle argue was about me. When my dad said "no," or put something off to another day, my uncle would say, "No, she's doing it today. Just let her do it today. Tomorrow's not guaranteed to anybody." The battle between them was very dramatic, because my uncle was older, and he was a lot chubbier than my dad. So, it was a battle of wisdom. I was also taught by him to question everything. There was no such thing as a wrong question. Their answers would be different, with great wisdom in both answers. When I was around both of them at the same time, my dad looked up to him, and sometimes when I asked my dad a question, he would direct the question to my uncle. So, both of us were learning.

After the passing of my uncle, my dad shut down. Oftentimes, he would just randomly ask what I missed most about Jah-Jah. I told him what I missed. He said he missed the same things. I've never seen my dad cry until that day. And I've never seen my dad silent. My dad was silent for a whole month. I would say even more. Even when someone spoke to him, he would just give a yes or no answer. There was no music. There was no talking. But he was very comforting. I believe that my uncle's passing brought my dad back to a humbling place, because I noticed that after my uncle's passing, he didn't go right back to the streets. He kind of took more to his family than the streets. I believe he took heed to his brother's advice to be there for his children daily. My uncle told him, "Your friends are here. If something needs to be done in the streets, you have enough friends." And that's what my dad did—his friends were doing more than what he did. I didn't understand what people knew about my dad, because I never saw that side of him. I knew that they were doing stuff, but my dad was a different person at home, even in my high school years. My dad made my breakfast. My dad made sure he was there, to the point where he was picking me up from high school. Every day, while driving home from school, he used to ask, "What do you want to have when you get in? Cabbage sandwich, corned beef sandwich, or egg sandwich?"—Uncle Jah-Jah used to ask the same question about dinner. And even if he went out, he was back in the morning. After some time, he admitted to me that he had learned from my uncle that when your children are eating, you should be in their presence. While they are eating, you should feed their mind as well. You should sit with someone while you're eating, so you can also have a conversation to nourish your mind. I then realized that these were the same principles at my godmother's house—we had to eat together. Family was very important to Jah-Jah, and that's why he always wanted to be with my dad; he didn't want him to be alone. Growing up in a community in Jamaica, everyone was like brothers. So being around his friends was also important to my dad. Their troubles became his troubles, and it was hard to let go of the streets.

I then turned into the nurturer for my dad. "Oh, are you okay? How was your day?" And even though I only got short answers, I was okay with it. I started to cook. I used to. I was never allowed to be in the kitchen, but my homework table was in front of the kitchen door, so I would always be looking in. *The first time I stepped into the kitchen, I was hesitant. However, I was able to replicate my dad's meals.* He was shocked and impressed. He gave me a thumbs up with a smile, and even asked for seconds. I had to be there to make sure he had something to eat, because he was not the same person. At one point, my dad ended up sleeping in my room. on the floor. I asked him why, once or twice, and then I just stopped asking. Then, one day, he just stopped. My uncle's passing and my dad's silence led me to be independent, and it led me to take on roles and gain tools that I still use today, because if not for my uncle passing, I probably wouldn't know how to cook. I love Uncle Jah-Jah, and I miss him dearly.

CHAPTER SEVEN:

CRACKS IN THE FOUNDATION

I've never said it before, but my mother didn't have custody of me after a while. Helen had full custody of me, and my father had temporary custody of me. My father was new to Canada, so he didn't have all his credentials. He only had his name on the documents as "Temporary Shared Custody," which involved Helen. The reason my mother didn't have custody was because she was still young and trying to do her own thing, out and about with her friends. My dad was concerned about how she was raising me. Sometimes my mother would do my hair, and other times, my father would pay for me to go to the hairdresser. I never learned from her how to cook. I learned my baking skills from Helen, who would bake every Sunday, and I would lick the bowl clean when she was done. And I learned how to cook from my dad. Helen also taught me a little bit about seasoning meat, but again, I was so young at the time that I just wanted to go play. I mostly inherited my cooking skills from my father and my Uncle Mark.

Helen got custody of me when I travelled back from New York. My mother and I had lived in New York for a period of time with my aunts. While in New York, I won a baby pageant, which Aunt Hazel had entered me into. It was called "Hollywood Babies," and there were thirty other babies. The photographer took black and white headshots of me. Afterwards, my aunt sent the pictures in, and I ended up in the top ten. They took more professional photos, and then the top ten led to top five, and I eventually won. New York is where my dad first saw me, before coming to Canada. When we returned to Canada, after the pageant, I was about to turn two, and the courts documented that Helen had custody of me. The prize money became a topic of discussion within my family. I received the money when I was seventeen years old, after I went to Covenant House. I had to send in some paperwork in order to receive the funds. I did not do it right away, however. I had to be reminded a few times before I mailed off the paperwork. I bought my first car, a Toyota Corolla, and gifts for my aunt with that money. I sent most of the money to Jamaica, where I had opened an account and deposited one thousand dollars. And then I basically gave her back the money, and it was mostly spent in Jamaica.

Aunt Hazel didn't have children of her own; that is why she was so involved in helping to raise me at that time. When I was born, it was a fight amongst my family members about where I should go and with whom. Everybody wanted me to be with them. I have pictures of myself as a child with three different sets of family members, wearing the same outfit. That's because I had to visit all three families on the same day, no exceptions. Everyone wanted to see me.

I resemble my mother. I have her shape. She has naturally curly hair. She's about five-feet-four, and she has the mouth of a soldier. People say I take after her in that regard. She's feisty, but she's a very intelligent woman. While growing up, she was at the top of her class. Her father was a policeman, and he was promoted to chief of police in Jamaica. Her mother was a nurse. My grandmother would say she was a very rebellious child. Even in her adulthood, she was very stubborn. She loved her own way.

My mother loved company. She always wanted to be around people, whether at parties or while shopping. I think that is a part of the reason why she was unable to nurture me and spend time with me. The woman had nice taste. My mother changed her furniture every year. She liked nice things. She liked furs at that time, so she bought a luxurious fur jacket that reached her ankles. Even if she was just going to the grocery store, she was well-dressed.

My mother is well-spoken, and she prefers using extensive vocabulary. I always admired her for being well-spoken and well-dressed. She taught me many things. She taught me to make sure when you leave your house, your bed, washroom, and kitchen are clean. When you wake up in the morning, you should make your bed, so everything is in order. She used to say, "God is a God of order. So, it's order for you to brush your teeth, wash your face, and spread your bed." She used to iron everything. My mother even ironed her pillowcases. It was so annoying. My mother and father were both from the streets, like an urban Bonnie and Clyde. But my mother was more of a fraud, and she had knowledge of drugs. After Sunday dinner, she used to grab her weed. She would roll it spliff by spliff, and she had a cigarette case with red and green flowers that she would put them in. I never witnessed somebody selling drugs until I was exposed to her dealings.

My mother never showed me love. Her way of love was basic—you have food, you have shelter. That's it. In my entire life, my mother has only hugged me twice. Having me in her youth meant she didn't have the level of preparedness that she needed to love me. So, I went without maternal love as a child. As I grew and recognized that her treatment was insufficient towards me, I would plead with her, saying, "Please don't treat your other children the same way you treat me. I was dragged up, but please raise these children properly."

My mom also worked at an insurance company, so she would get dressed every morning and go to work. Nobody knew about her secret, hidden life of crime. It was all revealed once she finally got caught. One time, I was travelling across the border, and I was stopped by the authorities at the border. They began to question me intensively. An officer asked, "Have you thought about what we told you before?"

I said, "Excuse me?"

The officer replied, "We've stopped you before and spoken to you."

I said, "You spoke with me?" I was using my old-school, red and white health card with no picture on it as a form of ID. They brought me to the other room, and I was really confused. Then they pulled up a picture, and after having a good look at the photo, they realized it was not me. When they showed me the picture, I didn't flinch. I recognized my mother in the picture. Instantly, I realized she had used my name and ID when she had gotten caught with weed at the border. She had forgotten she had her cigarette case on her. They asked me to identify the person in the picture, and I said I had no idea who it was. After this happened, I wasn't allowed to enter the United States for a while. When I confronted my mother about this situation, she denied it. I didn't have the evidence to show her at the time. She wanted to argue with me instead, and I told her that she shouldn't have done that. I inquired further, "Why did you use my name at the border in the first place? And why do you have a second set of my identification?" I connected the dots, realizing that I had two sets of birth certificates: the original and the new one with my name change. She had the original, but I didn't know that. This was the window that showed me my mother's life of crime. I now understood that my mother was living a double, or a triple, life, but I never questioned her about it.

I got a phone call one night from my aunt, her sister, telling me to come for her kids. I said to her, "But it's late in the night. Why should I come and get the kids?"

She replied, "The police have arrested your mom."

I said, "What?" I hesitated at first, and then I responded, exhausted, "I don't know what's going on, and I don't want to be involved in it." I kindly asked my aunt if she could go for the kids, but she lived far away, so I know that would have been hectic for her. Therefore, I offered to pay her cab fare. I told her they'd give over the kids if someone who looked more mature than I do showed up. I was of age, but I thought it would have been better for an older adult to be present. I then three-way called my godmother, and I said, "Okay, well, Mom is in trouble. And if someone doesn't go for her kids, they are gonna end up in the system." My godmother was in Newmarket. There was no way she was getting to Toronto at that time. My aunt lived in Scarborough, so I said, "Okay." We hung up with my godmother, and she relayed me back to the officer that was there. What happened was my mother's boyfriend lived in the same building as her. So, the kids were in her unit, but the incident that took place was in her boyfriend's unit. What happened was that the police came, they entered his house, and my mother ran into the washroom. In that moment, she became scared and fled from the cops, hiding in the washroom. When they opened the washroom, the police officer fought with her to the point where she was bleeding, because she failed to comply with their orders.

The officers thought that they had messed up big time as well. He took my godmother and spoke to me. He asked me if I lived there, where I lived, and when the kids arrived there. He said there were two children there. It was my brother and sister who, at the time, were about six or eight years old. The officer was concerned enough to imply that I phone someone to come for them before another officer got on the scene. That way we could quickly clear up that part, because my mother was hurt. "That's the most we can do for you at this time. We won't call Children's Aid at this moment. But if the other officers get here, they're going to want to do that. So, get someone to come in fast and save the children." Lo and behold, my aunt ended up getting there. Based on her current position and past history, there was no way the police would have given her the kids. So, I told my aunt to take the cab and I'd just pay for it. I'd reimburse her the following day. And I'd come and see her the following day as well. My mother ended up telling her that there was some money in her purse. She could use it to take a cab back home or stay the night. My aunt actually ended up staying the night with the kids at their home, in that apartment. Funny enough, my mother's boyfriend was released, because it was his first charge, even though it was his domain. When they went to court, he ended up getting bail, but my mother didn't get bailed, because she had a bigger charge of importing. At the same time, she was also quite sharp with a police officer. They had broken her nose. So, the police officer offered my mother a healthy amount of money not to show up at court. And she contemplated it. My godmother was at the courthouse, so it was relayed to me that outside the courtroom, they were saying, "We'll give her the bail." She went up to the court a couple of times. While she was in court, she said they saw that my mother needed medical help, and they asked, "How did you get this injury?" But she was very fluid as to why she got the injuries, and why he was paying her off. My godmother had told her "No," but my mother sided with the police behind our backs.

I remember my mom coming to my apartment. She told me that I would watch the kids while she went to New York. I knew that had to mean strangers, because I knew that she already had charges against her. I knew that she couldn't cross the border. I said, "Okay, I'll watch them. Whatever." It didn't bother me, and they were happy to be at my house for a weekend anyway. She dropped them off on a Friday, and she was back on Saturday. I said, "Why are you here?"

She said, "Oh, I'm not going to New York anymore." She took the children with her, and that's the last time I saw my mother before she ended up going to Jamaica with her two children, using the money. She never returned to this country.

At that time, you needed to have landed or permanent resident papers. What she did was take the money as a buyout, and she basically deported herself. That's what my godmother didn't want her to do, because she could have beat the charge, at least that charge. However, she would still have that importing charge. God willing, she'd beat that charge, or just do time, but she made a choice behind our backs, because we really thought she went to America. The school kept on calling my godmother and my aunt, saying, "The kids are not here. Where are the children?" We just kept saying that my mother had taken them to America. And then four months, six months, a year passed, and my mother was still in Jamaica with the two small children. I was now twenty-two years old.

It's been eighteen years since my mother's been in Jamaica. She never ever came back. Well, she wasn't able to come back, because she wasn't a citizen. She had her landed status, but she made her choice. Her new boyfriend went to Jamaica, and they tried to build a house, but he ended up taking her stuff from her house. So, she basically started off in Jamaica with zero. In the beginning, she would call and say, "Okay, I need you to call my bank and send me some money." And I would ask, "Where's the payout?" To which she would say, "Well, you know, I tried to build a house, and that money's gone."

My godmother was very upset with her, because she ran away from a charge and now, she couldn't come back. Now she was basically wanted. I never laid eyes on my mother again until a year ago when I went to Jamaica and I met up with her. During the time of her being in Jamaica, we only had simple conversations, whether it was wishing her Happy Mother's Day or Happy Birthday. We'd argued a few times over the phone, until the kids reached out to me and said they wanted to come back. I asked if they knew where their IDs were, but they couldn't find them. It was difficult to try to get them back, because we couldn't prove that they were Canadians.

My younger brother, Nat, always went through a rollercoaster of emotions with her. When my mom decided to leave Canada and go to Jamaica with her two kids, he wasn't a part of that plan. I know that my brother was very upset that she had left the country without taking him. I said to myself, "I have to protect him. We are in this together." Nat and I were born in the same month, and we had similar attitudes. He was amazing at basketball, and he was over-smart, if you asked me. Although I knew he had his own emotions to deal with, I made it a point of duty to always be there for him.

My mom and I had an important conversation after my grandmother on my dad's side passed away. She called me and said, "I'm really sorry for the way I treated you, growing up. I apologize for the way I dealt with you as a child. I could see that you were just wanting to be nurtured, but I was unable to provide that. The reason I treated you that way was because I felt as though you stole the love that your father used to give to me. After we had our first kid, he stopped showing me love. It was never the same. No matter what I did, I could never get it back." She continued, "Even when I entered the drug world to impress your dad, it still didn't fool him or shake him. All he cared about was you. I never received a proper kiss from him, ever again. You were born." So that explained the verbal and physical abuse. I thought it was stupid, but I knew she had repressed so much anger and resentment towards me that all she could do was hurt me.

CHAPTER EIGHT:

REBUILDING THE FOUNDATION

When I was in middle school, a boy from my school had a liking for me. His name was Vone. I was surprised, because I was more tomboyish. After my time in the States, I grew a little more fashionable and started to incorporate some feminine clothing into my wardrobe. My aunt helped with this transformation. Eventually, he and I became close, just through conversations and hanging out. He was a handsome fellow. He was athletic, and he played soccer. His family was well-known in the community as well. We grew close quite quickly. Long story short, I became pregnant. When I found out, I was in a state of shock, because I was just starting to make money. I was getting deeper into the game, and pregnancy and street life don't mix. My biggest issue was how to tell my dad. I didn't tell him at first. Quite frankly, I didn't tell anybody at first. At this time, I was still on the volleyball team. I ended up telling my boyfriend and, of course, he was ecstatic. I then mustered up the courage to tell my dad. Surprisingly, he wasn't disappointed. His main concern was, "Are you going to finish school?"

That's all he cared about at that moment. I assured him that I was going to continue my education. I told him I was six months pregnant. When I revealed this to him, he burst into laughter. Then I joined him, and we laughed together for a while. It was a funny moment, because I was coming home every day as if nothing had changed. At that point, my dad became more nurturing. He showered me with care and attention, because he wanted to be sure I was comfortable at all times. He knew my boyfriend in passing, but he made sure to find out exactly who he was. Soon after, I was at school during my spare period. My friend came running to me, panting and gasping for breath. I was hanging out in somebody else's class, minding my business as usual. My friend, who was now exhausted from running, burst into the classroom and said, "Your dad's outside!" I looked at the time and noted that school was not over. Usually, my dad picked me up after school. The time was late in the afternoon, but not yet 3:30 p.m. I quickly stood up and hurried down the steps. My high school had a big window at the end of the steps, at least ten feet of large windows. As I stood on the step, facing the window, I saw my dad wearing Clark's socks, jeans, a printed shirt, and a mesh undershirt. I stood there for a moment, processing what I was seeing. My dad was standing outside, holding a Bristol board poster that read, "Who is Vone?" My jaw dropped, as I thought to myself, *"No, he did not."* He carried on, and I stood there and crossed my arms, watching him, because I was so upset. I asked myself, *"Why didn't he just ask me? Why did he have to do this?"* A crowd was forming, because most people in my school knew who I was, and everybody recognized my father, because it was an area school. I thought, *"This is actually not funny."* As I felt myself getting upset, a group of girls passed by, laughing, and my instinct was to fight them, but I knew that I couldn't. Most people in the eleventh and twelfth grade had a spare, so they were already outside, hanging around the school. I went out to the yard and asked him, "What are you doing?"

He said, "I need to know who this guy is."

I said, "So why didn't you ask me? Why do you have to do this like you don't like him?" When he saw in my face that I was upset, he began to turn to leave, but I said, "No, I'm leaving now, too, because you've just ruined my day."

He said, "No, why are you leaving? Just finish your last class."

I told him he had already interrupted my day. By this time, I had walked away from him. There were three feet between the drop-off spot and the main doors with the big window. He returned to his car, and as people were passing by, he rolled down the window to ask, "Do you know Vone?"

I noticed this, and my frustration rose. I asked him, "Didn't I just tell you to stop?" I turned and hopped in the car, and demanded that he drive off, completely disregarding that my backpack was left at school. Of course, when I returned to school, it was all gossip and talk. But it didn't bother me, because I knew his heart, where it was all coming from. In that same week, I invited Vone over to our home, and he and my father spoke for a while. My dad asked who his family was, and when he told him, he knew who they were instantly. I breathed a sigh of relief, as I was worried that my father might have a problem with them. Luckily, one of Vone's family members hung out with my dad, and they weren't in any problems. They had a decent conversation. He asked him, "What are your plans? What is your age? Do you go to church? What's your religion? Do you work?" Of course, he worked. He had two seasonal jobs at the time.

I was liked by many boys, but they were the bad-boy types. I wasn't really attracted to the bad-boy type, because I knew what it came with. He had brothers and cousins who were also in the game, but he was nothing like them. He was very flirtatious. He was popular across the city for many reasons, but not because he was in the streets. He was also in a dance group. He played the drums for most school events, and was a star soccer player. We got along for the most part. He lived with his mother, uncle, and grandmother. I would go over there from time to time. At one point, I even started to stay over, and I eventually got attached to his family. His immediate family liked me. I always had my own place, and sometimes we would go back and forth between my apartment and their apartment. He would support me financially, even though I didn't really need it. It was just him stepping up and doing the right thing.

Dean was my first boyfriend. Although we didn't do a thing back then, we just hung out, went shopping, and chilled at the arcades. He lived in New York City, and he was one year older than I was. There were five of us that hung out, plus his nephew. A day came when I answered his home telephone, and a lady asked, "Who's this? And where is Dean?" I was not up for her attitude, and I gave it right back to her, to the point where I hung up the phone. She called back a few times before I answered again. This time, we went at it. I was cursing her out in Jamaican, and she was cursing me out with her heavy Brooklyn accent. She then asked to talk to his mom, who was not home at the moment, and her son Dontay. I then calmed down and said, "Oh, you're Dontay's mom. He's outside. I can get him for you." She said, "Yes, I am. And who the fuck is this?" Her swearing set me back off, and while we went at it again, she requested to speak with Dean immediately, because she was on a three-way call, and I was wasting her time. I went to call Dontay, and she talked with him in a nice, calm, loving manner. She then asked to talk with his dad, and he told her he was not home and would be back soon. I sat in the chair confused, and tried to put this confusing statement together. I had been around this child for over two years, and everyone took me for a fool. I went outside on the stoop and asked one of the guys we hung out with if Dean was Dontay's father. I got no response. In fact, they all started to walk away. I could see Dean coming up the block, but before he got to the house, I took out all my anger and past trauma out on his room. I broke everything that could be broken. I smiled and asked him how he could lie about his own blood. I did not give him time to answer; I just walked away and never looked back.

One day, I was sitting in history class. I asked the history teacher if I could use the hall pass to go to the washroom. Of course, I wasn't allowed, because normally when I took it, I didn't come back, or I took too long, and then nobody else could use the hall pass. But this particular day, I said, "I really need to use the washroom. I promise you; I will come back this time." She hesitated at first. I had asked because I felt a pain that came from my toe, and I knew what time it was. Only a few people knew about my pregnancy. My teacher was not one of them. I already knew she was going to say "no" to me, so I asked again in an extremely nice manner. I would normally just walk out, but I proceeded to ask nicely, three times. The fourth time, I was over it. I said, "I'm leaving. I don't care."

On my way out the door, she said, "Okay, here, take the hall pass in case a teacher stops you. But remember your first promise when you said you'll be right back."

I turned to her and said, "That promise is null and void, but I will be back." So even in pain, I was still being a smartass. I walked down the hallway, and my vice-principal stopped me. He said, "Blaire," and I interrupted him, as I held up my hall pass to validate myself. He asked, "How long have you had it?"

I said, "I swear, I just received it."

He said, "Why did you need a pass?"

I said, "To use the washroom."

He pointed behind me and said, "But you passed two bathrooms."

And I said, "First of all, it's not a bathroom. It's a washroom. And I don't want to use that washroom; I want to use the one downstairs." He said, "Okay, smart mouth."

I proceeded down the steps, crossed the street with ease, and I went through the Emergency doors of the hospital across the street. I went through the regular quarters of the hospital, to labour and delivery on the first floor. I looked around and turned to the first nurse I saw, and I said, "I'm having contractions. What am I supposed to do?" She looked up at me and said that I was calm. I said, "Can I not be calm now? Is it time to not be calm? Because I don't want to be calm any longer." She called someone and put me on course to the regular routine. I was nervous, and nobody knew where I was. So, I called my friend Tyson. I didn't say anything. She just said, "You're not at school." And I said, "No, I went to an appointment." I lied. Well, not exactly. She asked, "Are you sure you're okay?"

I said, "No, I'm fine." I didn't want anybody to see me in pain. I was usually very tough. Then I called Vone and told him. He thought I was joking at first, so I hung up the phone.

A young Black nurse came to my bedside. It seemed as though it was her first week on the job. She was kind to me. I had some other nurses, but this one particularly never left my side. She said to me, "The tougher you act, the tougher it's gonna be for you." I looked at her with a side eye, as if to say, *"Who are you talking to?"* Even in difficult times, I still played tough. I wasn't there for long. I'd say my labour was probably under five hours, because I was active. I had just gone to a volleyball game three weeks prior. I had my son around six o'clock in the evening. I also had a daughter that day. Twins. I had no clue I was pregnant with twins. The other baby did not make it, which made me feel as if I had done something wrong. I was still feeling worried and could feel myself getting dizzy. Immediately, I started to get anxious.

By this time, my friends were coming to visit. Then in walked my history teacher. She looked at me and said, "What do you mean you've been pregnant in my class this whole time?" I didn't even look up. She said, "Second of all, where's the hall pass?" I pointed to the locker with my stuff, and I told her where it was. She said, "Boy, you're really stubborn." Then the nurse came in. She said my babies were beautiful. While I was talking, I still felt myself getting really anxious, but I wasn't showing it. Nevertheless, the nurse noticed it. I had begun to sweat a little bit. By this time, I had the volleyball team and people from the community in my room. I hadn't seen my dad in a couple of days, but

I didn't find it weird that he hadn't come home. I had talked to him that week, once or twice. Then it clicked to me that I was anxious because my dad was not there, and Helen was not there yet. One of my cousins came to the hospital to see me. When she got close to my bedside, she whispered in my ear, "Your dad's in trouble." The dots connected; that's why I hadn't seen him. He was putting in double the time in the streets, so I did not see him for the last month of my pregnancy. We would talk on the phone, but I knew he was home because of the cooking. He was making money for me and his grandchild, even though I didn't really need it at the time. My cousin saw worry flash across my face and said, "Don't worry. He normally figures it out."

My anxiety skyrocketed. The nurses said my visitors had to leave. The young nurse asked me, "Are you okay?" I hesitated, and I said I thought so. She said, "You don't look okay. Are you sure?"

I said, "I think so. But I don't think so." Suddenly, I felt an intense wave of heat hit me. My body grew warm. Then I started to bleed. It was as if I was having the babies all over again. All of my visitors had left, and the nurse stood in my empty room. When I looked up at her, she was crying. She didn't know what to do; she was in a state of panic.

I just remember saying to her, "You'll be fine." I don't remember anything after that. I don't remember, because I went into a coma. I recall waking up in the ICU. I opened my eyes, and I saw a couple of my friends. I didn't see my dad, but I saw my godmother. My friend was crying hysterically. At this point, I didn't know what was wrong. I tried to move my lips and ask her why she was crying, but the words weren't coming out. Later that evening, the same thing happened. I opened my eyes and I did not know I was in a coma. There was no one with me in the hospital, just the nurse. I could hear her saying, "The same stubbornness you came in with, you have to use it to fight through, because your son needs you." I don't remember anything after that. I was in a coma for three months.

For the three months, it was routine that I would get up and talk to myself. I was basically having an out-of-body experience. I saw everyone who was coming in and out of my hospital room to visit me, and my outer-body self was happy. I thought to myself, "Wow, they came to see me," and "Wow, my mother came." But I still didn't see my dad. There was one incident where I saw my uncle and my grandmother at the door, because where I was situated in the ICU, I was probably about five feet away from the door. My uncle began to hum one of the songs that he used to sing when I was younger. I felt happy that day. I continued watching myself and listening to the conversations that were taking place around me. One of the conversations that took place was my mother saying that she couldn't bear to see me like this. The doctor said, "What do you want to do?" Then one of the nurses said, "But I don't think you're her guardian. Helen and her dad have to make the decision. You're not able to." So, my mother wasn't able to make the decision on whether to pull the plug that day. Even to this day, I ask myself, *"If she had the power, what would she have decided?"* The hospital called my dad. He eventually came, and there was something they wanted him to sign. However, my dad wasn't supposed to be in the country, so he was in hiding. His fear was coming to the hospital and someone seeing him and reporting him. One day, he sat by me and held my hand, and in that soft voice, he said, "Come on, we have things to do. I cleaned the house. I'm here now. I don't want to see you like this. Numero uno, I know you can hear me." Then he started to pray. At that moment, I know it sounds cliché, but it was over. I woke up! It was truly a miracle. The nurses, hospital staff, and my family and friends were all elated. The moment I woke up, they rushed my father out of the room, and the doctors came to check on me. At that time, I had only glimpsed my son once. Vone had him at the time, and my mom was assisting with taking care of him as well. I learned all of this information that same evening. The doctors monitored me for a while. My friends came to see me again. The other patients and visitors were extremely bothered whenever I had visitors, because, of course, we were loud. I had gotten fat because I was being fed intravenously, so my friends were making fun of me. I would try to laugh, but it was difficult, because I was still in pain. I didn't know I had high blood pressure, but that's why I had slipped into a coma. I ended up hemorrhaging, because my blood pressure was really high, and I didn't know so I used to eat everything. I was in the hospital for another two weeks. My doctor advised me that if I were to get pregnant again, it would be a high-risk pregnancy, so I should try not to get pregnant right away.

My son was amazingly cute. I brought him to school one day, and everybody gathered around to look, and coo, at him. Eventually, reality settled in, and I had to make a decision. The school year was not finished, so I decided to finish school. Everybody watched my son, mainly my dad. I barely pushed a stroller. Also, there was no contention with my mother. She would come, and she would bring him toys and clothing. She would also bathe him. However, my dad had a more prominent role. He would pick him up before sunrise and take him for a walk. My boyfriend's family was very involved, too. I basically just went to school. All our family members helped in raising him. Eventually, I had to stop my dad from taking him, because he was still in the streets. He promised that whenever he had him, he would not do certain things or be around certain people. His friends loved my son, as he was my dad's first grandchild.

One day, we went to a soccer game. There was tension on the field, and I'm not just talking about the game. I was with my dad and his two friends, and we took my son to the game. They never left my side; they felt as if they were protecting me and my baby. It was as if I had security. The game ended, and I suddenly heard "Pow!" It was a gunshot. There was a shootout, and my dad was furious, because I was present with my child in this dangerous situation. I ran and was able to get to the car, and as I drove out, the shootout continued. I got so upset with my dad. I told him, "This is why I don't want to be around you and your friends. It's always a risk! We can't even watch a game without the street life ruining it." I was extremely upset. I yelled,

"Don't come back here. You and your friends just go away!" That's the second time I ever saw my dad cry. I was livid, and I didn't care what came out of my mouth, because my child and I were in danger. Even though I ran him away like a dog, he would still come and get the baby every morning. I wasn't talking to him. I would pass the baby to him in silence, and he would bring him back and then he would go away. That happened for about a week before he was back at the house and things returned to normal.

At this time, my dad was still wanted, and the police came to my house more than five times in a week. No matter what questions they would ask me, I always said, "I don't know who you're speaking of."

They said, "You always give us the same song and dance." But they noticed I had a baby now. I always had a smart mouth with them. And they said, "Well, we need to speak to your dad about some stuff."
I said, "When you find him, let me know."

They said, "Kamelah, cut the bullshit. We've been outside, so we see that he comes here early in the morning." But the way the building was situated, they didn't know which way he turned. Soon after, my dad stopped coming, because I told him that they knew of his whereabouts. The police then said, "Well, we know you told him, because he stopped coming. Who doesn't want to see their grandchild?" My son was three months old at the time. For them to say that they had seen my dad in the early mornings meant that they had been watching him for a long period of time. My superintendent told me that they even came to him and asked whose name was on the lease. But he didn't live there, so, technically, the police couldn't come there. They always saw him at the balcony. They never saw him leaving my unit. This went on for about three months. They would come periodically. One morning, I heard a loud boom. It was the police, the fire department, and the RCMP. They wanted my dad, and they didn't care. They came into my apartment, and they tore it apart.

My furniture and carpet were destroyed. I had stylish mirrored furniture, and green and black leather couches. I had mirrored centre tables, a mural, and a black coffee table. They broke everything. As they broke, I cursed. I was still hiding money in the house, and they found it, but they didn't want the money. They wanted my dad. There was never a gun in my house, unless it was on someone. I didn't smoke weed. I didn't drink. So, what were they looking for? They didn't have to damage the unit to find a physical person. I lived in a one-bedroom apartment on the first floor. It wasn't hard to search. There were police on the balcony, there were police outside, and there was a fire truck and an ambulance outside. It was ridiculous. That went on for an hour or two while they questioned me, and I still didn't have an answer. To be honest, I really didn't know where my dad was anyway. I felt bad, because the only reason he had resurfaced was because I was sick. Of course, they apologized, but I didn't care. What I wanted to know was who was going to clean up the mess, and who was going to replace all the items they had destroyed. An officer gave me his card, and I told him I wasn't asking for a card. I was asking for a response. I said, "You guys have no manners with your big boots, walking up and down the house." They tore up cereal boxes, and they tore through my groceries. They tore through my clothes. I was devastated. I sat in that mess with my baby, and I cried. I cried because this was not my issue. It was really my dad's issue. I don't know what happened, or why this time they wanted him so badly. Truthfully, I had no answers. My first instinct was to call my godmother and go home, but I knew I would have to answer a lot of questions. I wasn't up for that. I eventually cleaned the apartment. The police officers did come back two weeks later, and they asked me where I had gotten my furniture from, so they could replace it. I had taken pictures, but back then I used a polaroid camera and had to get the pictures printed. I said, "This is not my dad's unit, legally, but you guys are doing the most."

They said, "We see that he's not coming around." So that meant they were still watching. And then the officer confessed and said that what they did was wrong, and that I could either tell them where I purchased the furniture from, or they could try and reimburse me. I told him, "F— off. I don't want anything from you guys. Forget about it." He insisted that what they did was incorrect. It was a big mess, and there were witnesses. Even some police officers were saying they had gone too far. I ended up fixing the apartment, but I wanted to go back home. However, I knew that if I went home, I'd have to answer to Helen, who thought I lived in Mississauga.

Soon after, I found out I was pregnant again. I told no one this time. My dad's friends were still coming by to check up on me, and then my dad's friend looked at me one day and asked, "Kamelah, you're pregnant?" I cursed him out and asked, "What are you talking about?" I didn't tell anyone for a long time.

The friend I called when I was giving birth was Tyson, my best friend at the time. She knew everything, and said nothing. I was the voice that would tell people off, even though I could also fight. She was the fighter. We lived in the same community. We always hung out with the same people. I mean, my friends that I had at the time were coming from the playground. We never left the community. Even though Jane street is broad, everybody knew everybody. Everybody's father knew somebody. All the children were friends.

Tyson was my friend, because I could tell her anything. She didn't know that I was home alone, but she knew my dad. She knew the lifestyle. The people that we hung out with were working for my dad. She knew that. She's now a Christian. Funny enough, we fell out for three summers straight. I lost the first fight. I didn't even know why we were fighting. Well, we had one last fight, and that was it. We went everywhere together. We did everything together. She knew what the streets were, but not on the level that I was in the street. She only knew of the streets. She was from the block. I was from the street. She liked the fact that I was from the street. We were inseparable. I don't know if she could sense that something was wrong with me, but if I was at her place and her mom said I had to go, she would say, "No, don't let her go." If she had five dollars, and I had zero, then she only had two dollars and fifty cents. If she had ten, she gave me five. You didn't see her without seeing me. It was actually the jealousy of other people that broke our friendship. It was just one incident that broke our friendship, and I found out recently that it was a lie. There was an incident when I was living alone: Someone knocked on my door. When I opened it, I knew the people at the door. I wasn't sure what they were doing there, or how they knew where I lived. When I stepped out into the hallway, there were about four or five other guys in masks. I asked what was going on, and they said they were sent to rob me. My apartment was fully furnished, and they said they had come for my dad's stuff. I said, "My dad is not even in the country. What are you guys talking about?" Then they told me that Tyson had told them to rob the place. I got angry. I looked like a cartoon with smoke coming out of my ears. I couldn't sleep the whole night. We argued, but I didn't let her know that I knew. I said to her, "I didn't go to my uncle's place yesterday; I went home." She asked, "What time did you get home?" Just by her reaction, I knew there had to be some truth to what they had said. The guys who came to rob the place knew that my dad had a philosophy: You have a base where you work, and you have a home. They thought it was my dad's base, but it was my home. There were six people in total, because there were five of them in the hallway, plus the person who knocked. However, I still couldn't believe it. This was my friend that I loved so dearly. How could she do this? But there are two sides to a story. We were still seeing guys in the streets, and they were saying, "Yo, your friend is wicked." So, we ended up arguing. And then I just slowly drifted away from her. She didn't know why. She thought my other friends were telling me things. We eventually fought, but she smokes, and I noticed that smokers get winded really quickly. The first couple of punches might hurt, but after that they're done. When we fought, I was hesitant, so I lost the fight. But then we fought again the next day, and then for two years straight. It wasn't until last year that I found out the truth. Someone asked me, "Do you still talk to Tyson?" And I said, "We don't speak. She's a Christian now." Then they asked, "Well, do you speak to Sarah?" And I said, "Why?" She went on to explain that Sarah had set the whole thing up, and had asked Tyson for my address so she could drop something off to my dad. So, they got my address from Tyson, but Sarah did the set up. Funny enough, when I fought Tyson, Sarah was there, on more than one occasion. When she asked what time I got home, she was only asking out of her concern. Almost nineteen years later, the truth was revealed, and I was out for Sarah's neck. But in due time I will deal with her.

I still went to school and went to New York City a few times with my son, Daiquane. I had my second child the next year, in February, on Valentine's Day. My dad and his friends came to visit me, and they stayed for a while before they got kicked out. I was mindful that what had happened before could happen again, so I tried my best to take it easy. I had the same amount of help as my first child, but not Helen's help. She came by and saw my son and said, "Tiny, you can't babysit for your friends all the time." Little did she know that I had two sons, and I was not babysitting at all. I broke the news to her when she got home. She begged me to move home, but I had other plans, and so did the Universe. Three weeks after having my second child, Jaiquane, I felt the same feeling and heat overtake my body, once again. I woke up two months later. This time, death's door was more like my grandmother and uncle talking to me and reminding me of the things I had promised to do in my teenage years. I arrived home to family and friends, even though a few were missing. I had a plan that I had to put in place, and it started with getting rid of some people.

I took five months off from school, but then enrolled in a computer college that was five minutes away from me. Most evenings after college, I would stop by our local grocery store. It wasn't that big, probably twenty feet in size, but each time I went there, there was an old Italian man who liked to engage in conversation. He mainly talked about the war, black civil rights, and stocks. Mario offered me his condominium, which was also in the Jane and Finch area. I questioned why he wanted to be so kind to me, and his answer was always, "You hold a good conversation, and you're highly intelligent. You have your children in a building that's not fit to raise them in. I have a young family living there at this moment." Their family size had increased, and he had given them a townhouse he had on the other side of the city. Mario requested that I come and see the unit that Thursday. I met him in the lobby, and he took me up to the ninth floor. Funny enough, this condominium was the same condominium that my mother had lived in the day she locked me up at the age of fifteen, so I was more than familiar with this building. The young family was also Jamaican. They went on to say how nice Mario and his wife were to them, as they had just migrated to this country. Lo and behold, I ended up moving into the unit the following month. Down the hall from me was a family friend I knew as a child from Down the Lane. A few floors down was Vone's mother. And I knew two other people who lived in this building from when my mother had lived there. There were two other buildings that faced the condominium. I had childhood friends—a pair of twins—that lived in the shorter building, and a few of my dad's friends that lived in the taller building. I became close to them again, as we would see each other in passing daily. I enjoyed the company of older people than young people. We got together sometimes, and partied together as well. While hanging out with them, I became a bit more popular, even though my childhood friends and I were younger than them, they still respected us and dealt with us fairly. They were also people in the streets. Velveen and Sharon were well-known in the dancehall community. I was only around them on weekends, as I was still going to school. Two other sisters, Michelle and Sangle, whom I knew from my childhood, would see me and the children daily, and stop and ask how I was doing. They also asked about my dad. I was respectful to them, as they also knew a lot of my dad's friends that were in the streets. Nevertheless, I would have my days when I didn't want to talk. I would see them at the local club each and every Friday, along with a few other people I knew from high school. My brother, Nat, would watch his nephews on some weekends, which he enjoyed, and they had a grand time while they were there. He took them shopping, and took them to the parks. He also allowed them to drive his car in the driveway, without the keys. From time to time, he would come over and spend a weekend with us. Partying became a routine, and also a distraction from my plan. I had to put this plan in place and fast.

CHAPTER NINE:

THE PLAN

Pep, my dad's baby mother, was a tall, dark-skinned lady. She didn't speak Jamaican at all, even though she was Jamaican. She spoke just as softly as Helen. She was a very organized person, and she was very kind. She was gracious enough to give me a lot of things, including clothes. While I was with her at her house, she would invite me to the kitchen. I told her my grandmother wouldn't allow me to go into the kitchen, so she took it upon herself to invite me into her kitchen. She wrote out rules, like a chart for the day, and my chores for the week when I was between thirteen and fifteen years old. She was very poised and was always well-dressed. She would correct you on the spot, and give you step-by-step instructions. She was a cleanliness-is-next-to-godliness kind of lady. She really liked to dance as well. I'm truly grateful for her teachings, even though we did not get along in the beginning.

Oftentimes, whenever I would think of something that I knew was not right, Pep or my Uncle Jah-Jah would pop up in my head. This would happen a lot, as I was putting together my plan. I had sent the children away for three months—Daiquane (DQ) went to Florida to my aunt, while Jaiquane (Showane) went to Jamaica to my Aunt Hazel. I sent them away so I could finish the school year.

I had a roommate at the time, whom I had known since I was eleven. She was going through a hard time with her mother. She also had a son, so I understood the struggles. I allowed her to stay until she got herself on her feet. My plan was in full motion. Only a few people knew what I was doing. In fact, the people who knew were my dad's friends and a young African guy named Frank. Frank was much younger than I, but when I used to pass by the park after school, he admired my dressing, which led to conversations. In regards to money, what Frank was explaining at that time I already had some knowledge of through my dad's friends. Frank's way was much different, and it involved much more money. I would ask my dad's friends questions with the knowledge that Frank had given me, and they would be confused, because it didn't quite go the way they were doing it. I finally took Frank up on his offer. He explained to me, "I don't want a percentage; I'm just trying to put you on the game, because I see that you're out here trying to do your best with two young children. Most people give their children away to their mothers for them to raise, so let's meet up next week, and I'll show you what's going on. We met over lunch. Frank's plan and my plan weren't the same in many ways, but the outcome was kind of the same, to say the least. We met a few more times, until I got a full understanding of exactly what was going on. I brought the information that I had, and put it together with the information my father's friends had, and the plan was made—I entered the world of fraud. My dad's friends idolized me, as I knew more than what they knew, and I educated them on what they were doing. They could make much more Frank's way. However, I never introduced them to each other. I worked with my dad's friends from city to city, from bank to bank, and still attended school. I would assist my roommate with the things she needed, as she was looking to move out shortly. When the children returned, I slowed down. I had enough money to do exactly what I wanted to do, but I didn't have the need to spend it. I just figured it would bring too much attention to me. Frank and I would contact each other from time to time. A few days after returning from a trip to Jamaica, there was a knock at my door. I looked through the peephole, and it was a tall, baldheaded, white man with a cigar in his mouth. His knocking became louder, so I opened the door. He said, "Good evening. Is Kamelah here?" Without hesitation, I said, "No, she's not. I'm just the babysitter. Is there something I can help you with?" He handed me a card and said, "Have her call me when she gets home." I said, "Okay, no problem. Have yourself a wonderful night," and I closed the door. I was confused. How was a police officer looking for me, but he didn't know who I really was? I looked at the card, and it just said his name and the division he was from. I put my plan on hold completely, as I was confused about what they wanted to talk to me about. In the back of my mind, I just thought it was something my dad had done again, or maybe they were looking for Goldy. Weeks passed, and I remained low. However, my dad's friend came to the building and asked me to come downstairs. When I got there, he seemed a bit upset, so naturally I asked, "Are you good?" He said, "Your roommate's in trouble. I don't know what to do." "What kind of trouble?" I asked. "Moreover, how do you know this?" He went on to explain that she got caught out of town in a bank. I was confused and frustrated, and by the look on my face he knew I had no clue what was going on or what he was talking about. He also had a surprised look on his face, as he thought I knew that she had picked up this lifestyle. So many thoughts went through my head. This girl was living in my house, rent-free, and I was coming in and giving her money, buying her stuff to get on her feet, and she went behind my back to my connect, to do some shit I knew she was not cut out for. I asked him how long this had been going on. When he uttered the words "two months," I gasped. With surprise, he said, "I can't believe she did this. I came here two months ago, and she was in the lobby. I asked her where you were, and she said you weren't home and that I should talk to her." Little did he know that I wasn't even in the country at that time. And little did she know that he wasn't my connect, as she had thought. Now more than ever, he was concerned. If she would write him, I could no longer vouch for her. I just told him to lay low and see what happens. Two days passed, and she came back, and believe it or not, I said absolutely nothing to her, and she did the same. I just let her know that I was giving her notice, as I was going to move myself. She was fine, or so I thought. The same bald police officer had come back three or four times, still asking for me while looking straight at me, and I gave him the same lie every time: "I'm just a babysitter." Five months passed, and my ex-roommate began to spread unnecessary lies about her charges, and tried to bring me in on it, which never made sense to me. We ended up fighting at our local grocery store, where I then revealed that I knew what was going on and, of course, she was shocked and tried to explain herself. It was way too late for that. Late one night, in that same month, I heard a knock on the door. It was the same baldheaded man, with no cigar and two other officers. I opened the door, and the slim one said, "Hi, Scarface. How are you?"

Scarface was a nickname the police had given to me from the cut my mom gave me over my eyebrow. If a police officer was calling me Scarface, then he also knew my dad. He asked if anybody else was home, and I told him, "No." Then he said he was placing me under arrest. I asked him "What for?" And he said, "Fraud." As I entered a room in the police station that had about four or five desks, I received a standing ovation, applause and all. The officer with the cigar announced me, saying, "We have Kamelah Blair, after all this time!" They placed me in a room, and another officer and a female officer came in. They read me my charges and my rights, and asked if I had a lawyer. I did, and I gave them his name. They looked up the phone number and, of course, I said absolutely nothing. The slim officer checked up on me from time to time. I felt as though I was there for a whole day, even though it was just a few hours. He asked if I was hungry, and I shook my head. He asked if I needed a medication, and even though I had asthma, I still shook my head. They took me outside to talk to my lawyer, and he just advised me to stay quiet, as he would be down there shortly. A slim officer, Scott, then came and sat down. He said, "I know you'll say nothing, but I have a gut feeling. I might be one of the rookies on the team, but I was taught to always go with my gut feeling." I just looked up at him and then put my head back down. He said, "I'll be back in five minutes. I'm going to take you to another room." He handcuffed me and waited for the female officer to arrive. We walked down the hallway and made a sharp right. He then advised me to stand in front of a doorway. In that doorway, I could see three to four desks, a few officers, and a lady in a chair turned sideways, sobbing. While the female officers stood beside me, Officer Scott went and sat in front of the lady. She was wearing a purple track suit, and her hair was long. He went on to say, "So if you see this person, you would know who they are?" She replied, while wiping her nose, "Yes, because she was my babysitter."

Officer Scott then looked at the female officer and gave her the hand motion to bring me in the room. I had no clue what was going on, but Officer Scott's gut feeling was right. Apparently, this lady had said that I had come into her apartment, taking her banking information without her consent. I later found out that she was sleeping with one of my dad's friends and wanted to get revenge on him. She went to the police, and by doing their investigations, they got a few pictures from the bank, a few fingerprints, and tracked me down. That was the reason for the standing ovation, because I was so hard to find. However, the timing never added up, because when it said I was in the bank, I was also in an accounting class in school. They couldn't figure out how I could be at two places at once, and I wasn't going to explain it to them. Officer Scott got mad at the young lady and said, "You're a damn liar, and I know it to be true!" He then handcuffed her and read her her rights. The female officer looked at me and said, "You're very lucky this lady has been here for hours stating she knew who you were, and by Officer Scott's gut feeling in bringing you down here, she put herself in way more trouble than you." My lawyer came about a half hour afterwards. They talked, and I was able to sign myself out, as I never had any previous charges. I went to court a month later, where a lawyer jumped up when my name was called and said they had a resolution for this case. We went outside and discussed it, and they gave me two months house arrest and two years' probation. I went from one hundred fraud charges to five.

CHAPTER TEN:

THE PHONE CALL

I was receiving phone calls from a strange number, and I would press "Decline." It wasn't a number I had seen or answered before. I was sitting down one Saturday morning and as a tradition, being Caribbean, I was cleaning up the house in the morning. I remember the day so clearly. I began to clean my room, and as I was putting things away, I passed my jewelry box. That jewelry box was where I kept most of the watches I had collected over the years. I took out a few and examined each one, reminiscing on the memory each watch held. I noticed that one of them had a faulty battery, so I sat down and fiddled with it. I was trying to pull it apart, when the same number called again. I answered and said, "Who the fuck is this? You really don't give up." I was frustrated with the damn watch, and the phone ringing again further annoyed me. I heard a familiar voice say, "It's me." I froze. Instantly, the voice flooded my mind with memories, and I quickly responded, "Where have you been?" He said, "I've been calling you for so long." I said, "You're calling from a strange number! You know

I'm not going to answer any strange numbers. Why didn't you text?" And he said he couldn't text from the number he was calling from. He asked me, "Are you good?" He asked about my kids, my dad, and a few of our friends. But by his voice, I could tell that something was wrong. I mean, he was happy to hear from me, but at the same time, I sensed that something was off. So, I asked again, "Are you sure you're good?" He suddenly said he needed a favour from me. His tone was serious, and I could sense the urgency in his voice. He continued, "I don't know if you're going to say yes. If you don't, it's fine. If you say yes, I want you to think about it again." And I said, "What could it be that I have to think about it?" And he said, "Well, I'm not around. But I need you to go somewhere for me. I need something. I can't go there, and I don't trust anyone to go there."

I said, "Well, okay, so what do you want me to do there? You know I don't like guns and stuff, and I don't do those kinds of things anymore. I'm not really in the game."

But he said, "Trust me. It's nothing like that. I just need something from a place, and I don't trust anyone to go there." I hadn't seen or heard from him for more than two years at this point. He'd been calling me for two years, so I said, "Sure."

He explained that he was going to let me meet a friend of his later that day. He said, "When you get there, you'll know the person, and they'll know you. So, they'll trust you to give you something that you need to get there. It's just an apartment, but I need the key. He has the key, and he doesn't trust anybody. I don't trust him like that either. I only trust you." I agreed. He continued, "When you get the key, you'll see a strange number calling. I'm not gonna call you back from this number. I want to call you back from the other number."

I said, "Fine." I got up, finished my cleaning routine, and began to get dressed for my evening excursion to meet his friend.

That evening, around seven o'clock, I drove a significant distance to the meeting spot I had been directed to go to. I spotted the friend, and he greeted me saying, "How are you? How's everything? How's the kids? I saw you in passing." He wasn't a complete stranger, as we had seen each other a few times at different events. He explained what he was doing. Then he said, "Frank said to give you this key." I took it and asked again, "So you're good?" And he said, "Yeah, you take care of yourself." I then turned on my heel and went my own way, back to the car. I waited for a little bit, and Frank called me and gave me the address. Then he told me that when I got there, I should just pack up everything in the living room. He would tell me where to drop it off. I said to him again, "Okay, this is weird."

He said, "Trust me. I don't trust anybody else, and I need it." I trusted him. I knew that he wouldn't put me in danger, but I was just worried, because Frank was on the scene. His friend was also African. And Africans are a tight-knit community. Frank said he didn't trust his friend, which was a red flag. Frank was much younger than I was, and he always respected me. I sat in my car, thinking over my next step. He sent me an address. I hesitated for a while, wondering if I should go right away or go the following day. I didn't even know what I was picking up. I definitely didn't want anybody to see me. I had put on a black tracksuit, grey-black Air Maxes, and a baseball cap—I turned it backwards. I borrowed my neighbour's car in order to remain untraceable and covert. She was fine with it. I decided I would go that night. I drove to the location and pulled up to a ten-storey building, located in a posh area. The neighbourhood at the time was very upper class. I used a key fob once I got to the lobby, and I held my head down, because there were several cameras in this upscale apartment. I went to the elevator and pressed the floor level Frank had directed me to go to. I got to the door, and the hallway was silent. It was as if everybody was asleep or had gone to work. I didn't hear a TV or a radio on the entire floor. I used the key and opened the door, and I kid you not, it was just one apartment full of money! I thought, "How the fuck am I gonna pick all of this up?" I walked in slowly, looking around, and the only thing that I could see on the floor was the doormat that was in the middle of the doorway. There was a border on the floor. The whole living room and dining room was littered with money. Cash everywhere. I proceeded to walk through, and I wondered how I was going to pack it all up. I remembered him saying to pack up what was in the living room and the dining room. I looked in the bedroom and observed that it was quite neat. The bed was well made. The dresser had the finest colognes and a couple of wristwatches sprawled on it. I didn't open the closet, although the door was slightly open. It was open enough for me to see the designer clothes hanging on velvet hangers. I then peeked into the washroom, and it was clean. I returned to the living room and stared at the abundance of cash. I sighed. I didn't know what to do. Suddenly, the phone rang. It was Frank. He was straight to the point. He said, "You don't have to count it, but I need it ASAP. There is a four-piece set of luggage in the master bedroom, in the closet. You can use it."

What happened next is a whole other story.

To be continued...

www.ingramcontent.com/pod-product-compliance
Lightning Source LLC
Chambersburg PA
CBHW070919080526
44589CB00013B/1366